Pupils in Transition

D0753670

Making the move from primary to secondary school is one of the major stepping stones in a young person's life. While there is a risk that some might find this move traumatic, there are many ways in which teachers can work to make the transition as smooth – and enjoyable – as possible. This book aims to help new and existing teachers to recognize the effects of transition, and to explore how schools can best ensure fluency at a time of change. The book explores the roles and concerns of the major stake-holders (the pupils and their parents, the Year 6 and Year 7 teachers), and shows that effective transitions must be firmly based on the continuity and progression designed into the National Curriculum, by the efficient and purposeful transfer of information between schools and by comprehensive liaison between the various parties involved. The book also offers specific advice about how to develop a transition audit, designed to help schools identify the strengths and weaknesses in their approach to transition.

Gill Nicholls is Senior Lecturer in the School of Educational Studies at the University of Surrey. **John Gardner** is Professor of Education at Queen's University, Belfast.

Pupils in Transition

Moving between Key Stages

Gill Nicholls and John Gardner

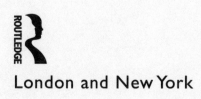

London and New York

First published 1999 by Routledge
11 New Fetter Lane, London EC4P 4EE

Simultaneously published in the USA and Canada
by Routledge
29 West 35th Street, New York, NY 10001

© 1999 Gill Nicholls and John Gardner

Typeset in Sabon by Routledge
Printed and bound in Great Britain by Cays Ltd, St. Ives PLC

All rights reserved. No part of this book may be reprinted or
reproduced or utilised in any form or by any electronic,
mechanical, or other means, now known or hereafter
invented, including photocopying and recording, or in any
information storage or retrieval system, without permission in
writing from the publishers.

British Library Cataloguing in Publication Data
A catalogue record for this book is available from the British Library

Library of Congress Cataloguing in Publication Data
Nicholls, Gill
    Pupils in transition: moving between key stages / Gill Nicholls and John
    Gardner
    Includes bibliographical references and index.
    1. Articulation (Education)–Great Britain. 2. Education, Elementary–
    Great Britain. 3. Education, Secondary–Great Britain. 4. Student
    adjustment–Great Britain. I. Gardner, John. II. Title.
LB 1626.N53   1999
373.18–dc21   98–25926

ISBN 0–415–17466–X (hbk)
ISBN 0–415–17467–8 (pbk)

Contents

Chapter 1

Introduction: principles and issues

This chapter introduces the concept of transition on which the book is based. The focus is on the transition from primary to secondary school or, to put it another way, from Key Stage 2 to Key Stage 3 where a change of school is involved. Three simple principles are identified: the importance of continuity and progression in teaching and learning; the need for primary and secondary schools to work closely together to deliver continuity and progression; and the need to recognize and ease the tensions and stresses which pupils can experience during the transition period. The majority of the chapter is given over to highlighting the issues that teachers and senior school managers on both sides of the transition must address.

Overview

In this introduction we provide an overview of the issues and set out the principles that govern good practice in managing transition. In one sense, the main transitions in a young person's development revolve around physical change and the development of social experience. These are the stepping stones of growing up and are entirely natural and inevitable. Young people progress at different rates and their families and communities provide the stabilizing and comforting framework for the various changes that affect them. This natural change-process contrasts with the formal and very much contrived transitions imposed by the social system in which young people are educated. Major transitions here include beginning school, changing from primary to secondary schooling, and eventually graduation to employment. Schools are the focus of this book and one of its main aims is to help new and existing teachers to recognize and accommodate the sometimes traumatic effects that such transitions have on young people's lives. A second aim is to examine how schools can best ensure fluent transitions, with a focus on transition from Key Stage 2 to Key Stage 3. It is widely accepted that this fluency should be underpinned by the continuity and progression designed into the curriculum, by the efficient and purposeful transfer of information at the interface and by comprehensive liaison between the various parties involved: teachers, pupils and parents.

In order to address the various issues we have adopted an approach which seeks first to identify matters concerning the main stakeholders: the pupils and their parents, the Year 6 teachers and the Year 7 teachers. Chapter 2 ('Pupils and parents in transition') therefore considers a pupil and parent perspective. Chapter 3 deals with the concepts and practicalities of 'Curriculum continuity and progression', while Chapter 4 focuses on 'Continuity and progression in the core subjects' (i.e. English, mathematics and science). Chapters 5 and 6 ('Transfer of information' and 'Liaison between schools, teachers and parents') respectively consider the various information requirements that exist and the mechanisms schools may use to increase the likelihood of success in transition. These chapters also deal with the elements of professional mistrust and even lack of respect which fuel what we have termed the 'phase conflict' between primary and secondary schooling. Much of this aspect of the work is drawn from the views of the many teachers with whom we have worked in a variety of research contexts.

The second aspect of our approach, making up Chapters 7 and 8, is to offer specific advice, illustrated by examples of good practice, on how the needs of children in transition may be met by teachers and schools. Chapter 7 ('What is happening in your school?') develops a 'transition audit', designed to enable schools to identify their strengths and weaknesses in their approach to transition. Chapter 8 ('Collaborative networks for continuity') takes this a step further to provide guidance on setting up the school networks and liaison processes that will govern a more system-wide exploitation of the continuity and progression, which the curriculum implies and indeed demands.

Principles

- Pupils should experience continuity and progression in their teaching and learning across the primary/secondary transition.
- Primary and secondary schools, associated by virtue of the transfer of pupils between them, should ensure that the necessary information transfer and liaison procedures are in place to ensure the continuity and progression in learning to which pupils are entitled.
- Primary and secondary schools should jointly recognize the difficulties and fears which pupils experience on changing schools and should work to lessen the impact of them.

These principles of curriculum continuity and progression and of professional collaboration across the transition 'divide' underpin the whole of this book. The issues giving rise to them, and arising from them, are not new. True, they are given more impetus by a curriculum that is designed to be seamless throughout the compulsory education age range and which seeks to enable children to learn, and be taught, at their own individual levels. The theory is idealized: a centralized curriculum, taught in differentiated fashion according to pupil needs, continuous across age and phase boundaries (e.g. primary and secondary) and assessed according to a standardized process. It is all so logical that the non-educationalist might just wonder what could possibly go wrong. Maybe it is not a case of going wrong, more a case of constantly seeking to reach the ideals – with a few hiccups and difficulties along the way. Sir Ron Dearing put it this way:

> A concern often expressed during the recent review of the National Curriculum was that there was a loss of momentum in pupils' progress between the end of Key Stage 2 and the beginning of Key Stage 3. Primary schools often felt that their achievements were not recognized and that secondary schools did not take sufficient account of the progress that pupils had made. Secondary schools, on the other hand, have to plan for pupils coming from a range of different primary schools and ensure that the curriculum in Year 7 builds on what may be a wide range of experience. This is not a new problem, and we need to make progress towards its solution.
>
> (SCAA 1996)

Dearing focused on the central problem: the discontinuity in the progress children make as a result, essentially, of changing schools. He proposed some underlying reasons: lack of recognition of primary work by secondary schools and the often wide range of incoming pupils' experience which secondary schools, sometimes with large numbers of feeder primary schools, have to accommodate. These issues in themselves hide deeper concerns and problems that we intend to draw out for scrutiny. For example it will be interesting to explore why some (or is it many?) primary schools might feel their achievements are not recognized. Might it be because they are looked down upon by their bigger cousins? Or might it more simply be that some secondary schools do not actually disseminate the transfer of information to the Year 7 teachers? Whatever the case, we intend to assess the perceptions of both the Key Stage 2 and Key Stage 3 teachers and then to propose ways of dealing with any divergence or lack of consensus between the sectors.

Pupils and parents in transition

Issues
- Which school will we choose?
- How will 'big school' be different?

These opening questions summarize the issues confronting pupils and their parents as they face a change in schools. The central issue for parents is to find the best school for their children. Once it has been chosen, and the pupils have been accepted, they and their parents then have expectations and perhaps doubts and worries associated with the prospective new environment.

We cannot avoid starting with the pupils. The children are the focus of all of these developments and their perception of the Key Stage 2/3 transition is very different from that of their teachers who manage the change routinely every year. 'Going to "big school" ' is a major event for pupils and indeed their parents. The rigmarole of choosing the school, or in an increasing number of cases undergoing a selection process for particular schools, is becoming more complex and stressful. As funding becomes increasingly tied to pupil numbers, schools are marketing themselves much more aggressively than ever before. Glossy brochures, open days and even 'special offers' of free items of school uniform or stationery are all trotted out in attempt to counter falling rolls or simply to compete with the school 'up the road'.

Caught up in all of this are the pupils, pushed by peer pressure to go 'where my pals are going' or by pressure from mum and dad to go to the school of *their* choice. Somehow the decision is made and the big day comes; they arrive at 'big school'. No longer the big boys and girls of their previous schools they find themselves in a relatively noisy world of hustle and bustle where everyone is bigger than them! The static classroom of yesterday is often replaced by a trek around a variety of rooms during the school day. The sense of isolation is intense as the sheer size of the school separates them from the familiar faces that might have come with them from their previous school. And the teachers! Instead of one teacher for almost everything, they find they have anything up to a dozen or more: perhaps a dozen different teaching styles, a dozen different personalities and even a dozen sets of classroom rules. For the first couple of weeks, they experience a whirlwind of change and unfamiliar practices until at last the main patterns of 'big school' life take shape and meaning and they settle into the compartmentalized curriculum of the secondary school.

They all survive of course...all of us who have been through the system know that. Today's schools are much more alert and ready to reduce the tension – and in some cases fear – that incoming pupils are apt to experience. Indeed many schools seek to exploit the awe and excitement that the pupils have by making the first few days special. Various events involving sports and group activities are provided to make a positive first impression. The secondary schools will often stagger the first day back for older pupils to enable the young ones to settle in without the added dimension of lots of larger, perhaps noisier and certainly at some level intimidating older pupils being around.

Curriculum continuity and progression

Issues
- Why continuity?
- What prevents continuity?
- What does a 'fresh start' mean?
- What is progression?
- How may continuity and progression be ensured in the core subjects?
- Teachers' perceptions of KS2 and 3 continuity
- Pupils' perceptions of subject continuity

Continuity and progression are uncompromisingly twinned in the National Curriculum. A central aim of the design is the progressive learning of children, a continuous building up of achievement and understanding limited only by the pupil's own capacity to learn. Such progression needs a curriculum which is operationally continuous and which allows children to position themselves, and be positioned by their teachers, according to the level of their own learning development. The programmes of study underpin this objective by detailing the learning experiences and content that every child is entitled to during each Key Stage of their schooling. Although a very blunt measurement device, the eight-level assessment scale provides a basis for reporting progress within these programmes of study. It is designed to make assessment information meaningful and amenable to education experts (teachers etc.) and non-educationalists (pupils, parents etc.) alike. Chapters 3 and 4 take these concepts of continuity and progression and consider how the theoretical design can be realized in the reality of today's schooling.

While few doubt the benefits of a continuous and progressive curriculum design, the argument that a change of schooling is a major and necessary transition, which is not unduly undermined by a discontinuity in experience, would certainly also find its supporters. Proponents of this view would argue that we should not underestimate children's adaptability and the importance of fostering such adaptability for later life. In so much as children are known to adapt quickly to changes in teaching and learning styles, without any detriment to their ultimate progress, the proponents of this view argue that a little discontinuity at the start of a major phase in children's education could even be beneficial.

Such a view, of course, does not deny that the continuity of the curriculum is re-engaged when the children have finally adapted and the school is fully addressing the Key Stage 3 agenda. On balance, most teachers and theorists would argue that continuity is a desirable ideal both from a teaching viewpoint (facilitating children's learning from where they are rather than from some arbitrary curriculum point) and most importantly from a pupil's perspective. Therein lies the rub of course. How does a Year 7 teacher manage to identify where to 'start' at a class and individual pupil level? Our experience would indicate that the latter issue – dealing with individual rather than class learning needs – lies at the heart of the matter. Once the levels of achievement of their pupils are known to the Year 7 teacher, supporting their progression properly will rely heavily on the teacher's competence in differentiated teaching.

Generally speaking, Year 7 teachers receive groups of young strangers that for the most part do not know each other and indeed might be coming from qualitatively different educational and perhaps social backgrounds. In attempts to make classes homogeneous in ability, many secondary schools use standardized tests to stream or band their first form intake; and many of course do not. Ability is, however, only part of the story. Differences in levels of attainment are likely to have less to do with their ability than with the nature and quality of their primary schooling. For the Year 7 teachers the notion of a 'fresh start' is therefore an attractive way forward that enables them to keep their own teaching fluent – to the detriment, perhaps, of any semblance of continuity for many of their individual charges. Yet, as we will show in Chapters 3 and 4, even this concept of fresh start has a number of qualitatively different interpretations, some of which arise from the nature of the subject concerned. This issue will be illustrated by the core subjects English, mathematics and science, which as a group offer several distinct variants.

The existence of mistrust or lack of respect for one another's judgement is a major factor in promoting discontinuity in the transition from primary school to secondary school. For the most part it is the secondary teachers, primarily in Year 7, that are perceived to ignore or disparage Year 6 work. For some years, in some quarters, there has been a perception of lower standards in primary schools, in the sense, for example, of the interpretation of a Level 5 performance in a primary school being at variance with the perception of a Level 5 performance in a secondary school. The settling in of the twin axes of teacher assessments for the process-based attainment targets in English, mathematics and science and the external assessments for the 'product' attainment targets may well see this divergence recede. However, the underlying professional mistrust may linger in other ways unless liaison on continuity and transfer begins to erode this 'phase conflict' also.

While some of the problems will be based on ill-informed or unprofessional attitudes among secondary teachers towards the quality of primary school work, there are also some relatively objective issues. Perhaps the most obvious example is the case of science where academic arguments still continue about the extent to which Key Stage 2 should be given over to the study of science. At the heart of this issue, is the perception of a lack of resources and a concern about the competence in a specialist area that a generalist primary teacher can bring to bear on the Key Stage 2 science requirements.

Primary school resources for science are unlikely ever to reach the quality and scale of those available to secondary schools (laboratories, dedicated technical support etc.) and in terms of staff competence, the current system of teacher training is unlikely to shift significantly towards specialist degree training for primary teachers. The nature of the primary curriculum and its delivery (i.e. the common model of one teacher per class) cannot demand the level of expertise in any subject area that specialist teaching in the secondary sector demands and expects. Add to this the very real differences between trying to provide a science practical lesson for a large primary class, compared to doing it with a relatively small secondary science group, and the causes for concern among science teachers become understandable.

Despite the strides being made in ensuring continuity in curriculum design, secondary teaching therefore remains very different from primary teaching. The pedagogic techniques themselves may be experiencing a growing convergence (for example a stronger focus in both sectors on greater pupil participation and learning autonomy) but the structural differences remain large. Secondary teachers usually teach several classes, often across two Key Stages and often in a moving cycle of rooms on the one hand and perhaps short-term modules on the other. Primary teachers, in contrast, usually teach the same class in the same room all of the time. Secondary teachers will see individual classes for a matter of hours each week, taking some months to familiarize themselves with each pupil's individual attributes and needs while their primary colleagues may accomplish the same level of familiarity within weeks. Secondary Year 7 teachers receive pupils who are experiencing a relatively traumatic change in circumstances (changes in school, teachers, friendships etc.) while Year 6 teachers, at the start of each year, receive pupils who are changing their one and only teacher – an albeit major yet comparatively lesser transition. In terms of briefing themselves on their new classes, the Year 7 teachers have to refer to transfer documentation while in many cases the Year 6 teacher can access detailed information and even pupil work, literally 'next door'.

Transfer of information and liaison between schools, teachers and parents

Issues
- Who knows pupils' strengths and weaknesses?
- What information has to be exchanged?
- What other types of information are available?
- Can the information be exchanged in electronic form?
- How should transferred information be used?
- What should liaison set out to achieve?
- How should liaison be organized?

Primary and secondary schools can clearly work together to ensure smooth transitions in the more affective dimensions of the change (easing pupils' and parents' worries etc.) as well as in the technical aspects of the change-over (progress information, continuity etc.). One aim of this book is to assist schools and teachers in thinking about how best they can achieve the desired approaches. If we accept the logic of curriculum continuity in the Key Stage 2/3 transition then we must seek the means of ensuring that the physical breaks in the process (changing schools, teachers etc.) are mitigated by strong liaison and information transfer processes. In these Chapters 5 and 6, we will examine how the best practice can work and what aspects of the process are most prone to failure.

Clearly the most important people in the transition from primary to secondary school are those teachers who guide the pupils through their last year of Key Stage 2 and those who welcome them into the first year of Key Stage 3.

For any one pupil there is generally only one teacher who sends them on their way to Key Stage 3. This Year 6 teacher will have taught them almost exclusively for the whole of their last year in primary school, and indeed in many cases perhaps the year before also. Inevitably, there will have been a strong bond between the teacher and the class, a bond founded on a complex mixture of teaching style, personality, whole class interaction and individual attention.

Few would argue with the proposition that the Year 6 teacher really knows the pupils; their strengths and weaknesses, likes and dislikes. Consider the variety of sources of information that they might have available to them: end-of-Key Stage 1 standard assessment tasks (SATs) and teacher assessments (TAs), end-of-Key Stage 2 SATs and TAs, portfolios of pupils' work, Key Stage 1 and 2 reports to parents, records from parent–teacher meetings and in many cases standardized literacy and numeracy test results. There will probably be a wide variety of teachers' personal records and in some cases detailed individual education plans (IEPs) or special needs audit profiles. It would seem desirable, then, that the information these teachers have should go forward in some suitable form for use by teachers at the next stage.

The rich information, which every Year 6 teacher has, can find a variety of vehicles of transfer to the secondary school. In some cases these are informal, e.g. through liaison visits by the primary teachers to the secondary schools, or vice versa. In other cases they are more formal with more expansive transfer reports detailing pupils' achievements, strengths, weaknesses and any special factors such as sporting or extra-curricular activities. There is a question mark over all such information, of course, especially where it strays into reporting the social side of pupils' experiences. Details of unusual domestic circumstances or perhaps minor behavioural lapses can be argued to be potentially prejudicial and even, for example in the former case, irrelevant. On the other hand, the 'fore-warned is fore-armed' argument also has its strong proponents.

In most cases some form of information does go forward and it is unlikely that secondary schools will experience the problem of having no information. By the same token, what they receive will rarely comprise the full range of information that is available. If there is a problem, it is more likely that some of the information that is transferred will be unnecessary or what is passed over will not contain the information perceived to be the most important.

Very often the packaging of the information itself can present unintended problems. If a Year 7 English teacher has to peruse a weighty portfolio of test results, class work and personal statements for each pupil, just to find the level of writing they are judged to be at, then the potential for the information transfer to be ignored or inadequately accessed must be increased. Basic information is required to be exchanged on so-called 'transfer forms'. These detail the pupils' performance in English, mathematics and science and they represent the very minimum of transferred information. While not required to do so, schools are also encouraged to send the additional information which they receive from the externally-conducted end-of-Key Stage 2 testing programme (namely the actual test scores, separate levels in English for reading and writing levels etc.).

Another dimension of the information transfer issue is the question of perceived value. Several types of experience lead to a degree of disillusionment among Year 6 teachers and these centre on the way in which they perceive their work to be accepted by their Year 7 colleagues in the secondary schools. Their main informants, curiously, are not their secondary peers but their own ex-pupils. For example, having worked hard to prepare many of their pupils to Level 5 in, say, mathematics they may then find their ex-pupils casually recounting a 'boring' first year of repetition and low-level work, often as low as Level 3. One reason for this type of serious discontinuity might be the Year 7 teachers choosing to start at the lowest level in their endeavours to cope with an intake which invariably has a wide range of educational experience and achievement. Year 6 teachers have no difficulty in accepting that a number of primary schools can feed the same secondary school and that there is therefore the potential for varying standards of entry experience and achievement. But, they argue, does the National Curriculum not encourage differentiated teaching of pupils at different levels? From the Year 7 teachers we might hear the understandable response: 'Easier said than done!'

Until comparatively recently the transfer of information between schools, and between schools and the local authorities, has had to be largely paper-based. Now, however, there are significant moves being made to enable more schools to transfer information electronically. Information technology has a huge potential for facilitating the transfer of information and liaison between schools.

The major benefit of most information systems available to schools is that they are fully two-way – i.e. they greatly facilitate exchange of information. They have the potential of enabling the Year 6 teacher to provide secondary schools, relatively easily, with all of the statutory information and much of the other information they hold themselves. For example, the scanning process involved in making a computer copy of pupil work to illustrate a teacher assessment in creative writing is now relatively simple and quick. Provided that the information is sufficiently structured, an information system will then allow access according to the users' requirements (and, of course, their right of access). For example, the mathematics teacher looking for mental arithmetic scores or the year head seeking to identify quickly all those with a notified medical condition are equally easy to facilitate in today's school administration systems. One clear benefit to all authorized users is likely to be the ease of access to accurate data.

Of course, the success of any such system will depend heavily on the reliability of the information fed into it. In Chapters 5 and 6 we examine how issues such as value-added assessments of secondary schooling depend on accurate and comprehensive entry-level information. With advances in administrative information technology for schools there is the clear prospect of heads of departments being able easily to access information about incoming pupils. Armed with a convenient and accessible information system, they will then be able to plan how best to resource the tackling of individual pupils' difficulties, perhaps through extra tuition, special emphasis on certain topics etc. Indeed possibilities are opening up for schools to become more reactive to individual needs and, dare we say it, increase the perception of their worth as institutions in a league table context!

A major aspect of improving transition processes is the quality of interaction (i.e. liaison) between the phases and between the schools to and from which the parents and pupils are 'in transition'. Chapter 6 specifically considers the main issues that good liaison arrangements can address, based on the shared goal of ensuring the smooth transition of children from one school system at Key Stage 2 to another at Key Stage 3. The chapter begins by setting out the general objectives for liaison, focusing squarely on meeting the needs of pupils by describing how schools might develop an effective approach. The different interfaces to which schools must attend: liaison with the transferring pupils, with the pupils' parents and with colleagues in partner schools, are dealt with in turn. Issues of resourcing a liaison programme, including choosing the liaison teachers and making provision for joint events between schools, are also considered. Professional liaison (between teachers in the partner clusters) is viewed as vital to a successful programme and suggestions are made for the types of contributions the various teachers involved can make. These are primarily the Year 6 and Year 7 teachers but designated liaison teachers, heads of core areas, heads of lower school etc. will all have important roles in providing the liaison structure that will ensure the parents are well-informed and the transition process is smooth.

What is happening in your school?

Issues
- Conducting an audit of existing transition arrangements
- Identifying the key personnel in the transition context
- Identifying areas for change and/or improvement

Everyone in a school is part of the transition process and no-one can be absolved from some commitment to supporting it. Even the Key Stage 1 or 4 teachers should acknowledge some responsibilities: in the one case for ensuring that the formative information from early years is recorded and in the other as representatives of the next stage in progression that the pupil will undertake. However, the key people remain the senior managers of each school, the heads of departments of the secondary school and the Year 6 and Year 7 teachers in direct contact with the pupils. Therein lies one of the most serious problems of the liaison process – the potential numbers of people who can provide and who need to receive information.

The typical situation is one of a secondary school receiving pupils from any number of primary schools within the general catchment area. Aside from the statutory information transfer (standard test and teacher assessment levels in English, mathematics and science) it is highly unlikely that any additional information will arrive in a common form...unless of course the secondary school has successfully set up liaison and information transfer procedures with its feeder primary schools! Chapter 7 focuses on these procedures and primarily on the needs of the secondary school end of the transition. A stepwise process for identifying who needs information, what information is needed and the extent to which any current arrangements fulfil or do not fulfil the needs, is also set out.

Collaborative networks for continuity

Issues
- Setting up and managing a collaborative network
- Team approaches to transition arrangements
- Establishing a calendar of events

Setting up a collaborative network requires school managers to be contributing at several levels and stages. Management input is vital to ensure that the network has authority and credibility and a variety of school-level policy and resourcing issues needs to be agreed at headteacher level. Working groups need to be organized to identify what needs to be done and to propose how it may be achieved. Chapter 8 discusses the issues involved in setting such teams up including who should constitute each team, and what objectives they should seek to achieve. Once the needs and objectives of the network are known, the next stage is to implement a working framework and calendar of events within which the various schools can strive to achieve the central objective: ensuring continuity and progress in the pupils' educational development. It is argued that the success of any transition network will be promoted by a sense of common purpose, mutual respect and frequent contact between the partner schools.

Chapter 2

Pupils and parents in transition

Issues
- Which school will we choose?
- How will 'big school' be different?

From a pupil's perspective, and that of their parents, these two questions summarize the major issues. Finding the right school is clearly the first priority. Moving to that new school at the primary/secondary transition stage is a very complex process and from the pupils' perspective it can be daunting and confusing. This chapter explores the influences and impacts that the prospect and the reality of the new environment hold for pupils.

Choosing a new school

At some point, probably in Year 5, children in primary schools become aware that soon they will be moving on. Members of their family and friends, at school and in their neighbourhoods, will probably be the first people to raise the subject. Parents today tend to ask their children which school they might fancy going to rather than simply directing them. This recognizes the autonomy we value in our children but it also allows other significant influences, such as the peer group, to have more of an impact on choices than perhaps we might wish. Peer group pressure can never be underestimated. If all of Emma's friends are going to Thorncliffe High is she likely to opt for Chertsey College?

Not that this implies that the choice of school is always simply left to Emma and the vagaries of peer pressure. What is more likely is that the parents will have done their homework and will be hoping to steer Emma towards the school that they think is best for her. In time-honoured fashion, a subtle – and perhaps on occasions not so subtle – process of making one school more attractive than the others gets under way. If the school in mind is not the school Emma fancies, she will inevitably experience the worries of making a choice, an important choice which will govern the next five or even seven years of her life. Most eleven-year-olds do appreciate the importance of making the right choice, even if it does appear that they are treating the matter as less important than music, fashion or football! When they are actually focused on discussing the choices, they will generally rehearse the conventional concerns about getting good results, having good facilities and being taught by good teachers.

The most influential information source for potential new recruits will be their peers, pupils at the various choice schools. Much of this information may appear to be relatively trivial. For example, the number of times PE is offered per week or particularly popular (or unpopular!) teachers may well be very important to the decision-making process. The schools themselves are well advised to send representatives to potential primary feeder schools and to offer orientation visits to promote the facilities and environment they can offer prospective new pupils. Some of these activities have become very sophisticated in recent years, with custom videos and glossy brochures being used as promotional warm-ups before the visits to and from the primaries take place. The pressure comes of course from the need to ensure self-preservation – a need that arises from a funding model based on enrolments that are influenced by public perceptions which themselves are fuelled by league tables and the publication of Office for Standards in Education (OFSTED) inspection reports. It might not be completely fair to say that the efforts made by secondary schools are driven purely by this self-preservation motive but many of the steps taken to recruit entering pupils patently push the most attractive aspects of the secondary schools involved. These include the science laboratories, technology rooms, gymnasium, computer rooms and so on. If they are over-exaggerated it is not uncommon for Year 7 pupils to express the view, some months into their first year, that they had been misled into thinking that such facilities would be playing a greater part in their schooling than was the case in reality!

A complicating factor for many pupils, and one that is increasing in its importance despite the recent change in government, is that the school they might want to go to, or that their parents might want them to go to, may operate a selective policy in recruiting new pupils. If the children find themselves in a selective school's catchment it is likely that peer pressure will include all the extra ingredients of selection-testing...tutoring, cramming etc., and the inevitable sense of failure that creeps in if the school of their choice does not accept them.

Going to 'big school'

The first issue to which schools and teachers must attend is the fact that pupils experience a degree of trauma in changing schools. For the vast majority, trauma is too strong a word – or is it? To what extent do we as teachers take into consideration the reality of the pupils' experience of changing schools? The most comparable experience in adulthood is beginning a new job. Finding the new job is the first set of experiences which cause stress, but once we have it we then arrive in a new location and are confronted by a new set of circumstances. Unless you are the sort of person who is naturally gregarious and who fits into the social processes and work routines first go, you will probably, for the first while at least, feel isolated, exposed and uncomfortable. You will rely very much on your new colleagues and those involved in overseeing your work, to induct you into your new role.

Pupils entering a new school are certainly no different in these aspects of their new circumstances and they are arguably vulnerable and exposed to many additional influences and processes which are potentially problematic to them. These might range from 'traditional' initiation rituals which frighten the life out of them to an unfamiliar form of lesson timetabling which leaves them lost and confused.

Recognizing the problems that pupils face, then, is the first step to providing a good induction programme for new entrants. This chapter seeks to remind us of the areas in which pupils do experience the various emotions which collectively can cause discomfort or, if adequately accommodated, can enable a smooth transition from the primary to the secondary school. The issues are discussed in terms of the contexts – social, physical, teaching and learning – in which they experience them.

The social context of the new school

Once into the secondary school, the new Year 7 pupils inevitably face a culture shock. Having recently been the seniors in the primary school, they now find themselves cast very much as the juniors in the hurly-burly of a noisy, complex and usually very much larger organization. The sense of being lowly first years is emphasized in every interaction, particularly with older pupils but often with teachers also. Clearly the former is difficult to control but just as clearly, all teachers must ensure they have a welcoming manner – whether they teach the first years they encounter or not. The effect of the perceived lack of status will quickly recede of course, as most of the pupils find and assert their position, but there will always be the few who are slower to settle and who may need a continuing eye kept on them.

Another feature of the new social context for many pupils is the sense of loneliness they may feel in their early days. For some the isolation and lack of familiar faces can be almost terrifying, while others who are naturally more gregarious will set about making new friends immediately. Teachers must be vigilant and should look out for those who are a little out of their depth, discreetly seeking to draw them into the social aspects of the class and school. One very simple but effective strategy on the teacher's part is to use the pupils' names as soon as possible to reduce the 'You, boy' or 'Yes, that girl over there' anonymity of the early days.

The physical context of the new school

One of the most striking changes for the primary-school child entering the secondary school, is the sheer size and structure of the new school. If the pupils have come from an open-plan primary, the corridors and classrooms may well be almost claustrophobic for the first while. There will probably be specially designated areas, perhaps at quite a distance from each other, such as the science laboratories, the gymnasium, the art rooms and the library. Instead of staying in the same room all day the pupils will find that they have to manage a complex timetable of as many as ten discrete subjects in different rooms throughout the day. Some of these rooms will be relatively spartan utility classrooms and some will be specialist rooms festooned with visual resources, other pupils' work or even the unfamiliar trappings and equipment of physical subjects such as technology or science.

The teaching context of the new school

The first day of a full timetable may make a significant impact on the new pupils. As many as ten teachers will lay down different sets of working rules and routines. Some will be subject-related (e.g. health and safety issues in the laboratory), others will more to do with the style of teaching and classroom management of the teacher concerned. Almost without exception, there will be a sense of awe as the class prepares to meet its next new teacher and it is incumbent on all Year 7 teachers that this awe does not turn into foreboding or downright fear! The 'Don't smile until Christmas' adage is not appropriate for these first moments; the best teachers will be business-like but welcoming, without any sacrifice to later control.

It may be some weeks, even months, before the pupils get used to the existence of so many new teachers and settle into this new compartmentalized model of schooling. The teachers themselves will not automatically appreciate this effect. They will probably have worked within a compartmentalized timetable for some years and the many new faces in front of them will be more of a class to begin with than a collection of individuals. Someone, probably the form teacher, must therefore take on the role of guiding the pupils through the complexities of the first few days.

The learning context of the new school

For some pupils from some primary schools, the learning context offered by the secondary school may be a major culture shock. The cosy, almost familial environment of the typical primary school may have accustomed incoming Year 7 pupils, relatively speaking, to an informal relationship with their teacher and an integrated learning environment that allows some choice of activity for the pupils and is generally conducted at a moderate pace. This idyllic situation is highly desirable for all schools, including secondary, but of course it is largely impractical for today's world. Even some primary schools, operating in a selective system, will find such an approach difficult as they force a pace that the preparation for selection tests may impose. Secondary schools, hampered by the very nature of an operational model that provides learning in short, time-bounded slots, have to deliver statutory programmes of study at a relatively brisk pace and in an order that allows very little pupil-choice in the nature and sequence of activities.

Generally speaking, though, the nature of learning in the secondary school will be more varied than in the typical primary school simply because more teachers are involved in each pupil's learning. On the one hand, those pupils who have developed personal autonomy in their learning, carefully fostered by their Key Stage 2 teachers, will probably meet didactic teachers who impose a passive 'receiver' role on them, characterized by much note-taking, pupil silence and teacher talk. On the other hand, those pupils entering the same secondary school but with a background of didactic teaching and passive learning in Key Stage 2, may just as easily find among their new teachers, those teachers who put them in the 'driving seat' of their own learning and who run highly participative and active classes.

Another ingredient in the culture shock of the new learning environment in the secondary school will undoubtedly be the resources for learning. These range from the scale of physical resources such as playing fields, science laboratories, technology blocks, computer suites etc., to the richness of provision within these areas and others such as the art rooms (e.g. photography, pottery kilns etc.) and the music department (e.g. electronic and traditional instruments). The much more formal segregation of the various subjects in the secondary timetable helps to increase the sense of specialism and a whole new range of subject titles such as information technology, home economics, French etc. will add to the pupils' sense of breaking away from the model of learning they experienced in primary school. The pupils' natural curiosity and sense of excitement in such a new environment will create an interest that the experienced Year 7 teacher will be ready to exploit.

The parents

In the hustle and bustle of the early days before school opens, and also in the early days of the first term, it is easy to forget the sense of, hopefully mild, anxiety felt by the parents of the pupils who are transferring schools. Parents who are sending their oldest or only child to secondary school will be particularly vulnerable to rumours of bullying, initiation ceremonies and homework overloading, and will 'casually' question their children on everything that goes on in the first few days. Seasoned parents, those with children already under way in secondary education, will have less trepidation but will none the less have some anxiety as their next in line makes the move to secondary school. The presence of parents and even grandparents around the school gates in the early days of the first term will give testimony to the worry felt and although it will generally be mild and largely unfounded, schools should nevertheless work to send positive, reassuring messages. In most cases a solid and thorough induction programme will settle the pupils and this will in turn settle the parents.

Summary

This chapter emphasizes the need to put pupils and their parents at the centre of any developments in the transition process. Their anxieties and expectations can be mollified and made realistic respectively by a committed effort on the part of the schools to provide timely and appropriate information on the transfer process. Schools, ideally primary and secondary schools working in collaboration, should therefore, for example:

1   formulate objectives and identify means of informing parents of Year 5 and Year 6 pupils about the transfer process;
2   inform and advise pupils and parents about the experience of secondary education and the expectations they should have;
3   introduce pupils in a positive manner to homework and discipline policies operated in the target secondary schools;
4   develop a strategy for informing parents about the secondary schools that are available, through various means including prospectuses, presentations from secondary liaison teachers and open evenings;
5   inform parents and pupils of teaching contexts in the secondary schools through samples of timetables, room maps of the school buildings, school handbooks and visits.

Chapter 3

Curriculum continuity and progression

Issues
- Why continuity?
- What prevents continuity?
- What does a 'fresh start' mean?
- What is progression?

This chapter considers what we mean by curriculum continuity and the relation this concept has to the progression in children's learning. Putting continuity and progression into practice is a task that requires a clear understanding of the practical issues involved and a teacher perspective on the various issues is therefore provided.

Introduction: the pursuit of continuity

The pursuit of curriculum continuity in the compulsory phases of education has been the goal of educationalists, policy makers and various other interested bodies for many years. The Hadow Report (1931), for example, considered that there should be no sharp divisions: compulsory education provision should be a 'coherent whole'. The equally famous Plowden Report, charged with examining the 'transition to secondary education', recognized that many secondary teachers 'involuntarily or deliberately repeat work that has already been attempted' (1967: para. 446). Other official reports followed suit (e.g. Bullock 1975) and in 1982 Cockcroft, in considering mathematics education, took the view that:

> the greatest problems exist on transfer to secondary school....These schools often receive pupils from a large number of contributory schools...the spread in mathematical attainment of these pupils can be very great and...it is not very easy to make sure that pupils continue their mathematical education at a level and speed which is appropriate.
> (1982: para. 429)

Derricott *et al.* (1985) reviewed the main reports up to the mid-1980s and summarized the design of a continuous curriculum as involving agreement on a series of core issues. These included the objectives of the curriculum, its content, the skills to be developed and the methods of assessment. The ideas and research eventually reached a critical mass, and in 1988 the 'National Curriculum' was born.

The planning for the national curriculum was unambiguous in its pursuit of continuity and progression:

> A national curriculum...will also help children's progression within and between primary and secondary education and will help to secure the continuity and coherence which is all too often lacking in what they are taught.
>
> (DES/WO 1987: 3)

And since its inception various representatives of the teaching profession have given it qualified endorsement, for example:

> In spite of continuing concerns about the traditional assemblage of subjects, and about curriculum overload, there remains a broad consensus on the structural benefits of the National Curriculum. It is seen as providing for continuity and progression and, with careful design and monitoring, as a potential source of coherence.
>
> (ATL 1996: 90)

This consensus on the structural benefits is relatively solid but many doubts remain about the operationalization of the system, particularly in the complementary area of the assessment of learning. The design is neat and tidy: a structured curriculum and a structured assessment scheme. Statutory *programmes of study* define the content of children's entitlement to learning in state-funded schools. These programmes are set out in four stages representing the *key stages* in a pupil's education (DFE 1995: v). Each programme of study is divided into several *attainment targets*, which are further divided into *levels* of attainment described by *level descriptions*. These level descriptions are used to report a pupil's progress along a continuous eight-level scale. The level descriptions are complex, multidimensional summaries of 'the types and range of performance that pupils working at a particular level should characteristically demonstrate' (DFE 1995: 25). The advice to teachers attempting to assess the level of their pupils' performance is to 'judge which description best fits the pupil's performance' and the complexity of the exercise is greatly compounded by the additional but clearly necessary advice '[e]ach description should be considered in conjunction with the descriptions for adjacent levels'.

Perhaps understandably then, and contrary to the perception of the curriculum itself, views on the assessment arrangements have remained largely critical. Large question marks continue to be drawn against such matters as the reliability and validity of national standardized testing; the amount of time being withdrawn from teaching and learning in order to facilitate the assessments; and the use of such 'blunt' pupil achievement measures to provide data for league tables of schools, based on their overall performances in the tests. Typical of the underlying concerns expressed is the professional unease with the eight-level measurement scale used:

> We need to start by recognising that the Levels are not empirically derived; they are not absolute forms of measurement. Like the 'ethos' of school, we cannot take snapshots of them or refer to them in any definitive sense. While we can say with confidence that at a particular point in time a child is exactly 1.5 metres tall, we cannot say with anything like the same degree of confidence that a pupil is exactly, or even nearly, a Level 3, whatever her or his age. Levels are socially constructed abstractions, developed from an unproven theoretical model of testing and created in the minds of test developers and the like. They should not be allowed to become their own – or the only – orthodoxy.
>
> (ATL 1996: 90)

Strong stuff, yet in the same report the ATL concede that respondents to their survey were beginning routinely to adopt the language of the levels, with pupils being described as 'only a Level 1' or 'a solid Level 5' and so on. Reliable and valid or not, the government's intended use of the levels is bedding in, and the School Curriculum and Assessment Authority (SCAA; replaced by the Qualifications and Curriculum Authority, QCA, in 1997) continued to promote their virtues, or at least those derived from the national external tests:

> The test levels awarded to pupils at the end of Key Stage 2 are based on standard national tests, administered and marked in a standard way. They therefore present a reliable overall picture of pupils' attainments at the start of Key Stage 3 and give comparable national data on which later value-added analyses can be based.
>
> (SCAA 1997: 3)

With a detailed curriculum, complete with aims, objectives and details of knowledge, skills and understanding to be assimilated by the pupils, and a structured assessment and reporting system, Derricott *et al.*'s vision of a continuous curriculum should be realized, should it not?

Confounding continuity

Clearly the national curriculum does provide a coherent framework for continuity in teaching and learning, but why then did OFSTED recently record the view that in science at Key Stage 3 '[t]eaching seldom takes sufficient account of pupils' capabilities and previous learning...' or 'seek[s] to build effectively on pupils' learning in Key Stage 2' (OFSTED 1995: 11, 14)? There are many reasons why continuity and progression may not be achieved and we shall examine some of them briefly below.

Planning by subjects

Brian Gorwood argues that our inability to deliver continuity from a curriculum designed to be continuous is largely due to 'fundamentally different philosophies of primary and secondary schooling' (1994: 361). In his view the fact that the National Curriculum was planned from a subject perspective makes aspects of its philosophy foreign to the perspective held by most primary schools i.e. more specifically meeting children's individual needs. Since at least the time of Plowden, he argues, primary schools have been striving to provide an educational experience that places 'emphasis on skills, attitudes and values which would eventually feed into the subject specific curriculum' (Gorwood 1994: 358). Thus it might be argued that the thematic and cross-curricular teaching, which is often encountered in primary school, is too distinct from the focused and subject-specific teaching of the compartmentalized curriculum in the secondary school. It is therefore possible that the curriculum is doomed to be operationally non-continuous, not because the content links do not exist – they do – but because the pedagogic links are not being made. At the heart of this problem lies the basic issue of communication between teachers in the two phases.

Teacher communication

In a report of her six-year longitudinal survey of science across the primary–secondary transition, Ruth Jarman despairingly noted that: 'evidence from this survey suggests that the establishment of primary–secondary links in science qualifies with honours to be included in that class of human activity described as "easier said than done" ' (1997: 309)! Difficult though it might be, it is abundantly clear that continuity cannot be achieved through simply ending a Key Stage 2 programme in one school and beginning a Key Stage 3 programme in the next. The programmes of study are not precise enough for cut-off points to be identified with any confidence and in any case the pupils themselves will be arriving with a variety of levels of accomplishment across the whole learning domain.

Secondary schools need to identify what the pupils have covered and learned in Key Stage 2 and, in advance of the pupils arriving, the obvious source of the information is the primary school. We will address the issue of teacher communication in Chapters 5 and 6 (*Transfer of information* and *Liaison between schools, teachers and parents*).

Overcrowding the Key Stage 2 curriculum

Right from the outset of the National Curriculum, complaints about the overburdening of Key Stages 1 and 2 arose frequently throughout the system. Problems were predicted and indeed were quickly experienced in areas such as overwork and stress among teachers, in-service training needs not being met, and the impracticality of trying to meet the curriculum requirements in the time available. Most importantly, primary teachers were predicting from the outset that time for basic literacy and numeracy work would be put under pressure by the demands of the overcrowded curriculum. Successive changes, and perhaps prime among them the simplification of the assessment arrangements, reduced the problems over a period of years but it was not until 1998 that the government signalled its intention actually to reduce the compulsory elements of the taught National Curriculum. In January of that year, the Secretary of State for Education, David Blunkett, announced that the compulsory subjects from September 1998 would include only English, mathematics and science with religious education and information technology. It has been proposed that subjects such as art, music, PE, technology and design, history and geography will not follow the KS1 and 2 programmes of study in these subjects between September 1998 and September 2000 (QCA Consultation letter, dated 13 January 1998). These subjects now appear to be reduced in importance with schools obliged 'to have regard to them' in offering a balanced educational experience for their pupils.

The motive for the change was not continuity and progression *per se*, rather it was to ensure that standards of literacy and numeracy could be raised by allowing more time than there had been for their pursuit. However the changes do mean that it is more reasonable to expect the Key Stage 2 curriculum to be covered in the time set aside for it – or is it? The time available for teaching remains restricted, to greater or lesser extents depending on the school, by the requirement to comply with end-of-Key Stage testing. In primary schools faced with the prospect of their enrolment being affected by a poor or even unremarkable showing in the 'league tables', there can be a considerable amount of time set aside to practise for external standard assessment tests (SATs) and then of course to administer them. 'You might as well stop teaching and start revising after Christmas' was how one teacher, though not alluding necessarily to any pressure to improve league table positions, viewed the situation in the 1995 ATL study (ATL 1996: 67).

The timing of the external tests usurps much of the Summer Term in the last year of Key Stage 2 but it can happen that the deadlines for completion of teacher assessments can also occur in the Spring Term. Strictly speaking this is stretching the definition of end-of-Key Stage; it is more like the middle rather than the end of the last year of the stage! In an interesting angle on the debate, the ATL (1996) has made the case for the level of attainment at the end-of-Key Stage 2 being assessed on entry to secondary school. After all, the argument goes, it is the receiving secondary school that has the most need for the information. The beginning of formal teaching under Key Stage 3 could perhaps be delayed to carry out the end-of-Key Stage 2 tests. Such a development, of course, would be heavily dependent on a quick turn-round of the external marking if the information is to be of any value to schools in setting and/or streaming their intake. Even if such a system could be organized, however, the end-of-Key Stage 2 teacher assessments would remain the responsibility of the Year 6 teachers.

Planned discontinuity

Curriculum continuity is a complex concept and curriculum *discontinuity* is not simply its exact opposite. For example if we were to say that continuity would always be desirable, it is not always true that discontinuity would be *un*-desirable. This ambiguity is an interesting educational phenomenon. Some would argue that the discontinuity inherent in transfer from primary to secondary parallels the physical and social 'growing up' of adolescence, and is therefore not necessarily a 'bad thing'. On the other hand, even if the argument tends towards embracing some aspects of discontinuity in Year 7 it will probably also demand that it be managed rather than simply accepted. Some managed or planned discontinuity may therefore be as desirable as planned continuity. For example, Key Stage 3 English teachers, aware of a relatively unsophisticated or underdeveloped reading programme in their pupils' Year 6, might plan a more challenging programme with a view to kick-starting an increased interest in reading. A sudden move to a wider range of genres may not immediately be perceived as discontinuous but it is representative of the kind of (hopefully positive) change in teaching and learning styles that incoming pupils can experience across the Key Stage 3 curriculum. Similar inherently positive discontinuities in learning experience might be encountered by Year 7 pupils in, for example, laboratory practicals in science or conversational lessons in French.

Unplanned curriculum discontinuities can generally be expected to be undesirable. They arise most often from gaps in the pupils' Key Stage 2 experience or from overlaps or repetition of Key Stage 2 learning in Year 7. Gaps in pupils' experience and learning may be caused, for example, by the Key Stage 2 teachers' lack of time to cover everything to the desired depth. In an overcrowded curriculum, the Year 6 teacher may choose to leave something out or to cover it relatively superficially. Teachers with mastery in every subject in the national Key Stage 2 curriculum must be very rare. It would not be surprising, then, if Year 6 teachers' decisions on what they teach in depth were influenced by their confidence, or indeed competence, in the subject area. Alternatively they may not like the subject particularly and will simply gravitate to the subjects they or their pupils find most enjoyable.

However they might arise, gaps in pupils' experience and learning present a real problem for teachers in Year 7 and many of them opt to provide a 'fresh start' for their new charges. Such a strategy, involving the potential repetition of Year 6 material, is seen as the lesser evil compared to trying to move forward from a position the pupils, or at least some of them, may not yet have reached.

'Fresh start' or 'follow-on'

All Year 7 teachers will recognize the idea of a 'fresh start' strategy and most would argue that Year 7 is inherently the beginning of a new stage in children's education. However the extent to which this new beginning builds on the pupils' previous experience and learning – a 'follow-on' that exploits the continuity and progression built into the curriculum – has major implications for Year 7 pupils. Research has shown that a 'fresh start' is also a complex concept with a number of variations. Anne Sutherland and her colleagues (1996), for example, identified several variants employed by some sixty-two Year 7[1] teachers and subject heads of department in both selective (grammar) and non-selective secondary schools. These may be summarized as:

- making the subject seem like new;
- a pre-determined level of attainment;
- nothing taken for granted;
- a clean slate, no prejudice or pre-judgement.

It would be inappropriate to generalize from such a small sample but Sutherland *et al.*'s work did suggest some differences between teachers of the three core subjects. For example, many of the mathematics and science teachers perceived sufficient differences in the learning experiences in the secondary school that a fresh start was the inevitable consequence. Within the two groups the reasoning behind this view did diverge a little though. The mathematics teachers viewed the general differences at school level to be particularly influential in their thinking. These included the compart-mentalized curriculum – separate subjects, taught by different teachers in relatively short but discrete time-slots – and the more homogeneous ability ranges that enable more whole-class teaching in the streamed classes. The science teachers, on the other hand, focused more on the subject-specific differences such as the laboratory environment and more involvement for the pupils in practicals and experiments.

In the same study the majority of the English teachers saw Year 7 as a combination of a fresh start and a follow-on. This was usually illustrated by a greater focus on literature but with a continuation in Key Stage 3 of the emphasis on basic literacy skills, begun in Key Stage 1 and continued through Key Stage 2:

> I am sure that the techniques involved here in the secondary school would be very similar to what they have been used to in primary school. But I think that is the very nature of English…[it] can lend itself to continuity…it is very much a recursive subject. You are dealing with language all of the time…adding to what they already know. Going back and reinforcing what you have done.
>
> (Head of English)[2]

Two central ideas were frequently expressed by the English teachers: first, English as a subject involves a long-term development of core skills; and second, the three attainment targets (Speaking and Listening,[3] Reading, and Writing) are inherently cross-phase and continuous.

Making the subject seem like new

This concept of fresh start has the objective of motivating and encouraging new pupils to develop an interest in the subject. Mathematics, for example, may be more vulnerable than English (with interesting books, role plays etc.) and science (with exciting experiments etc.) to pupils becoming jaded, perhaps as a result of lack of success or indeed by sheer lack of interest and boredom. Key Stage 3 teachers might therefore make a conscious effort to enliven the subject, distancing it from any previous bad experiences and making it seem new. Some of the strategies used by Year 7 teachers in the three core subjects to motivate Year 7 pupils are discussed later. This 'fresh start' strategy can be viewed as a planned discontinuity, perhaps incorpo-rating content continuity from Year 6 but with a deliberate attempt to provide a different (i.e. discontinuous) learning approach:

take something which they can do, something maybe new or approached in a different way and then at least they get success in it. And they suddenly begin to believe in themselves.

(Head of Mathematics)

A pre-determined level of attainment

It is possible to take an approach which focuses only on continuity rather than progression, and this version of continuity may simply be a pre-determined position – often at quite a low level – on the curriculum map. In this approach the teacher is oblivious to, perhaps uninterested in, what has gone before and how far the individual pupils have progressed:

> I really don't look at it as a follow-on from Year 7. I mean, I know we follow on as regards the curriculum, but I'm not looking to start where they left off at all...they haven't all done the same thing so basically we start at Level 3 in a certain topic.

(Head of Science)

Without doubt, Year 7 teachers who are faced with pupils coming from a variety of primary schools will also be confronted with a wide range of experiences and levels of accomplishment, regardless of the ability range of their new intake. Experienced Year 7 teachers will be able to predict some of the likely gaps and perhaps the general range of attainments. There is therefore a strong temptation, often based on long experience, to fix a point in the curriculum and simply start there. Most teachers who adopt this strategy will of course amend their own planning and teaching as pupils show their ability to cope with the material with which they are being presented. All too often, however, the simple way out is to accept the repetition that might arise in the cause of keeping everyone on the same topic or activity. Clearly this could lead to some degree of disaffection with those pupils who perceive Year 7 as a repetition of Year 6 work.

Nothing taken for granted

Pre-determining a fixed curriculum point, at which all of the pupils *will* start, is one strategy for dealing with varied educational backgrounds. Another is to assume nothing and to take the time to explore the pupils' levels of achievement before planning the teaching in detail. Sometimes this might be expressed negatively: 'we couldn't assume that the children had all been taught the same stuff or that they had covered it to the same extent...[so] we just assume that they don't really know anything' but perhaps the more usual view is that a period of finding out what the children can do, is what is needed:

In my group of 26 this year I have 11 or 12 primary schools represented. You might find in one school they've covered a great deal more
than in another so we need to begin by revising a lot of the ba-
sics...just finding where the children are at.

(English Teacher)

A clean slate, no prejudice or pre-judgement

This is an important dimension of a 'fresh start' that is perhaps distin-
guished from the others in being more pastoral than curricular. It does,
though, have a curricular dimension:

If you're told that a child isn't good at something, I'm not sure that's a
good thing. I think it's better to let them have a fresh start. I think
maybe I'd just like to treat them all in the same way. It usually doesn't
take very long to spot the children who have a flair.

(Science Teacher)

But it often refers to reports which might be forwarded from primary
schools on pupils' behaviour, attitude and so on. In the context of a
selective system, established in some regions and growing in others, it also
heralds a refusal on the part of the Year 7 teachers in non-selective schools
to accept labels of failure on their pupils: 'Everybody starts on a new
basis...we forget the passes and failures and all the rest of it from primary
school'.

Variable progression

The underpinning premise of the continuity which is designed into the
National Curriculum is that it be progressive. Not progressive in the
political or social sense, but based on some model of a pupil's increasing
knowledge, skill and understanding within a particular learning (subject)
domain. The underlying model is based on a notional 'typical pupil' and
the broad stages of education that he or she passes through. The complementary assessment model is even more fixed on a typical pupil. It is
specifically tied to a prediction of the level of attainment in the learning
progression that most children will have reached at particular ages and
times in compulsory schooling. All very fine if you are typical and fit into
the scheme of progression that underpins the structure of each programme
of study in its four Key Stages. But what if you are not typical, if you are
more gifted or less able than most? What of the child, irrespective of
ability, who suffers a period of extended illness with the result that the
whole progressive plan is stalled or even knocked backwards?

Differentiated teaching is the answer you will hear from the Establish-ment, with some platitudes to advise that you should have regard to planning how time and resources can be scheduled for the exceptional and not so exceptional needs. True, differentiated teaching is the answer but those time and resource concerns may well be insurmountable as the imperatives of a packed curriculum, even with recent reductions, drive the pace of teaching along.

Setting aside the difficult cases for a moment, there is a fundamental question to be asked about the progression of even 'typical' pupils. Is it in fact reasonable to believe that progression can be defined rigidly for the typical pupil in terms of Key Stages and the eight-level scale? In some respects, yes. Teachers have long experience of how children learn and how varied the patterns of this learning are. This practical classroom experi-ence, as Martin Hughes argues, is one method of generating a model for progression in learning. Working without any theoretical base teachers or curriculum designers can 'come to believe, as a direct result of their experience in the classroom, that pupils will learn more effectively if one activity comes before rather than after another activity, or that some learning experiences are more or less "appropriate" for pupils at a particular age' (Hughes 1994: 3).

This was largely the model used by the panels that were set up to create the programmes of study for the National Curriculum, following the Education Reform Act of 1988. How 'more or less appropriate' a model for all pupils is it? In *Progression in Learning* (1994), Hughes and others tackled a number of questions related to the concept of progression. Foremost among these was the extent to which variation exists between children in their levels of understanding. Although claiming no definitive answers, the work nevertheless highlighted some interesting issues. Of the five studies reported, two identified considerable variation between children of the same age while some children were outperforming others who were six or seven years older then themselves. This type of inverted lag was also apparent in the pre-school study reported in the same book (Munn 1994) and as a result Hughes poses the interesting question: 'Are the low-performing children simply trailing behind the others, or are they on a different route altogether?' If there are other routes, are the progres-sion models used in the national curriculum programmes of study appropriate 'more or less' for all? Again the answer has to be yes and no. Yes in the sense that some form of articulated progression is necessary to enable planning in schools and classrooms to proceed. And no in the sense that within this broad articulation of predicted typical progression, it must be recognized that not all children progress at the same rate or along the same route.

Although the main issue in this book is the cross-phase transition between schools, we must not forget that continuity and progression are required to be the hallmarks of the provision within schools; from Key Stage 1 to Key Stage 2 in the primary school and from Key Stage 3 to Key Stage 4 in the secondary school. Clearly before any school looks at their response to ensuring continuity across the divide they must first look to ensure that they are building progressively on children's learning within their own schools. Teachers will often say that they are doing little different under a national curriculum imperative: 'We had to write things down in a different format, with aims and attainment targets and so on, but I'm not teaching anything new that I didn't teach before' (English teacher), but they will probably concede that the formality of planning has meant that there is generally more discussion of whole-school curricular issues and not just their own immediate working contexts. With continuity and progression being addressed within a school, understanding of what has gone on in the previous stage, or the needs of the next stage, is likely to be more keenly developed.

Summary

This chapter has emphasized and justified the long sought after goal of continuity in the learning experiences between the two main phases of compulsory education: primary and secondary. Bearing in mind the important caveat that not all discontinuity is bad, the chapter challenges schools to:

1   recognize and attempt to reconcile the 'planning by subjects' approach to teaching in secondary education and the thematic and cross-curricular approach more commonly found in primary education;
2   develop cross-phase communications between teachers in each sector;
3   consider when a 'fresh start' or 'follow-on' is the better course of action in Year 7.

Notes

1   Sutherland et al.'s research covered eight clusters of secondary-level schools and their feeder primaries in Northern Ireland. The Northern Ireland version of the national curriculum has Year 8 as the first form of entry to Key Stage 3 schooling, owing to entry at an earlier age to primary schools in Northern Ireland. As this is identical to Year 7 in England and Wales it is reported here as Year 7.
2   All quotations in this chapter come from the study The Transition between Key Stage 2 and Key Stage 3 (1996) by Sutherland, Johnston and Gardner unless otherwise noted.
3   The Sutherland study was undertaken in Northern Ireland where, although almost identical in structure and content, the version of the national curriculum has some differences in terminology. For example the national curriculum process attainment target (AT1) in English, Speaking and Listening, is called

Talking and Listening, and the AT1 in science, Experimental and Investigative Science is called Exploring and Investigating in Science! For convenience these differences have been replaced by the England and Wales versions in the reports of this study.

Chapter 4

Continuity and progression in the core subjects

Issues
- How may continuity and progression be ensured in the core subjects?
- Teachers' perceptions of KS2 and 3 continuity
- Pupils' perceptions of subject continuity

This chapter considers continuity and progression within the core subjects (English, mathematics and science), and the relationship they have to pupils' learning. Continuity of learning in subject areas requires a clear understanding of the programmes of study at each Key Stage at the point of transition. The notion of a 'fresh start' in Year 7 compared to a 'follow-on' from Year 6 is discussed and the differences in approach that can arise in the core subjects of English, mathematics and science are explored.

Introduction

General perceptions of KS2 and KS3 teachers

Generally speaking, schools on both sides of the primary–secondary transition have become quite proficient in monitoring and maintaining continuity between their own transition stages (i.e. Key Stage 1 to 2 and Key Stage 3 to 4 respectively). However, the limited extent of communication between the two types of school has contrived to maintain a significant potential for discontinuity in children's learning experiences in moving from one to the other. Such a situation also leads to instances of professional mistrust, condescension and disparagement in what we would call 'phase conflict'. Rarely, it must be said, would these sentiments present themselves openly when teachers from the two sectors meet. Rather they take the form of perceptions (some based on personal experience) and even prejudices (some based on hearsay) which find comfort in some quarters within each sector. Sometimes they are accurate and valid but sometimes they are gross misrepresentations or over-simplifications.

Complaints of repetition in early Key Stage 3 form the bulk of comments from Key Stage 2. Often the complaints are not based on empirical evidence (e.g. visits to the schools to observe teaching or curriculum liaison meetings); they more often than not arise from comments from ex-pupils' parents or ex-pupils themselves on the occasional visits made to their previous schools. Such complaints will probably occur more in mathematics and science, where the content material is more tightly defined than in English and where the potential for a particular topic to be recapped is high.

In English the main area of repetition is often the choice of class novels. Clearly more of a possibility when no curriculum liaison exists, it nevertheless can happen deliberately when the Key Stage 2 school adopts novels that will be followed-on in the Key Stage 3 school. It has not been unknown for primary schools in selective areas to compete with others by promoting their compatibility with the grammar school by claiming the same reading list! Deliberate repetition can also arise when the Key Stage 3 teachers have decided that the novel in question is particularly important in their scheme of work. In both cases it is unlikely that all of the pupils in the Year 7 class will be from the same primary school and will have read the same books. The presence of even several such pupils will, however, raise the prospect of them perceiving their English work as simply a repetition. One way of reducing the impact of this is for such pupils to be given a sequel to the class book that they have already read (so long as one exists e.g. *Rebel on the Rock* for *Carrie's War*), with the request that they contribute to discussion of the class book anyway. By far the best strategies, however, are to find out what novels have been read, from the primary schools in advance or the pupils themselves as soon as possible at the start of Key Stage 3, with a view to ensuring there is no repetition of book choice.

With the more prescribed topic list for science and mathematics, it is reasonable to argue that a degree of repetition can have benefits both in refreshing and consolidating prior learning, and in providing a common base among the pupil group for more advanced working i.e. progression. Most Key Stage 2 teachers would concede that the common model of intake in a Key Stage 3 school is one of children coming from a variety of schools and therefore different educational backgrounds. Key Stage 3 teachers, as we mentioned above, cope with this problem in a number of different ways and some degree of repetition – new to some but a recap for others – is inevitable in the attempt to ensure the levelling out of the class. 'Yes,' some Key Stage 2 teachers will agree, 'but does it have to last as much as the whole first year and even further into the Key Stage 3 programme?'

There is the feeling that maybe they are taking the pupils and going down to the lowest common denominator...the feedback from past pupils is that they have been marking time in the first year...in mathematics and science...

(Year 6 Teacher)[1]

As we have said earlier, this concept of a 'fresh start' at a pre-determined level is a relatively common strategy for coping with a wide range of experiences and attainments in a Key Stage 3 intake class. Key Stage 3 teachers, however, should reflect on the impact such a policy has in terms of the Key Stage 2 teacher's perceptions of the situation. For Key Stage 2 teachers to bring their pupils to Level 5, say, only to hear that their first three months in Key Stage 3 has been at Level 3, is often tantamount to a personal slight – even though in most cases it would clearly not be intended.

Perceptions of pupils

Sutherland *et al.* have explored the views of Year 7 pupils in relation to the transition from their primary school to their secondary school. While their findings from interviews with forty-six groups of pupils (with between 4–6 pupils in each group) could not be considered generalizable to all Year 7 pupils, they are nonetheless of interest when attempting to identify the concerns and experiences of such pupils. One strong indication arising from the research was that the pupils considered that where they encountered repetition it often led to what they called 'harder' work. On probing this concept in the pupils' experiences of the three core subjects, 'harder' was recognized to be 'pupil-speak' that was used not to describe work which presented them necessarily with difficulty but for more advanced working within the same theme i.e. progression. In one instance in mathematics, for example, work on negative numbers may have appeared at first sight to have been repetition but in reality it was being extended in the secondary school to include subtraction of negative numbers. This concept of the subject being 'harder' was experienced in all three core subjects and indicates that while children may complain of repetition they do in many cases recognize that they and the learning they are undertaking are progressing.

In English, it is likely that similarities between the two phases in the work experienced by pupils will include a continuing emphasis on spelling, punctuation, grammar and so on: 'You are expected to write better sentences...use speech marks...and punctuation...and full stops...'. Lessons in Year 7 will tend to be more varied with longer and more frequent writing assignments including homework. More sophisticated or 'mature' writing will be expected: 'We would be expected to try to put our answers in our own words' and writing generally, particularly essays, will be the least liked aspect of Key Stage 3 English. Reading is likely to retain its attractions for those who already enjoy it, while a stimulating approach in the early days may well attract more recruits.

General oral work and more specifically drama-related work such as acting out poems and stories, improvisations etc. will usually prove to be very popular. The library and its facilities will also often serve as a new and important attraction in Key Stage 3 English. It is reasonable to expect that the greater variety of resources and facilities, and the perceived variety of activities, book genres, teaching styles etc., will continue to be an attractive element of secondary schools for incoming pupils. Key Stage 3 English teachers, if they don't already do so, should therefore ensure that they capitalize on the benefits that these can offer in motivating pupils.

The 'newness' of the teaching and learning environment and styles is particularly important in science where the laboratory and its attendant aura of mystery and excitement provide stark contrast to the science learning environments in most primary schools. The distinction between seeing demonstrations of experiments, a common experience in primary schools that have relatively limited resources, and actually doing them personally in the secondary school laboratory is important. Excitement is easily generated. For example, the possible dangers of Bunsen burners ('you feel more adult if you use flames and stuff...'), the complicated 'sci-fi' equipment, the secrets of life and the mystery of chemical reactions guarantee rapt attention in the early days, usually with sufficient continuing interest to maintain motivation well through Key Stage 3 and onwards. The Bunsen burner is often accorded pride of place in the science teacher's armoury; indeed it is often described as a rite of passage on entering secondary education.

We should pause at this point, however, and reinforce Ruth Jarman's view (1993) that pupils should not be encouraged to disparage their primary science once they experience the wonders of the fully equipped secondary science laboratory. Primary science cannot match the facilities, nor indeed is it likely that the teachers will have the subject expertise to be found in secondary schools, but it must not be forgotten that the primary classroom is the seedbed of the interest and quest for learning in science that most children bring to the secondary school. Secondary science teachers should therefore encourage respect for the strides being made in science education in primary schools.

Some of the experiments which are popular in primary schools relate to the areas needing the least complicated equipment or technology. For example, electrical circuit experiments, with batteries, bulbs, buzzers etc., and various 'fair test' experiments, involving time, weights etc., are widely used. Very often, however, even these types of experiments, with low technology equipment and low risk factors, are the subject of teacher demonstration: 'in primary school your teacher would do it...[the teacher] didn't think you were trustable but they trust you more now...[in secondary school] they let you make your own mistakes so you can correct them'. This independence in science will be particularly valued by Year 7 pupils in secondary schools, and practicals and experiments will remain the most popular activities. The least liked aspect will be writing in science and particularly writing the experiments up.

Repetition in mathematics in the early days of Year 7 may be a relatively common experience. This would be due partly to the definitive nature of the mathematics attainment targets and their subject content, and partly due to mathematics teachers choosing either to begin their Key Stage 3 programmes at a pre-determined level of attainment in the curriculum or to begin with a programme of revision of Key Stage 2 material to explore the pupils' levels of attainment. Repetition should not necessarily be viewed as a negative form of discontinuity. Pupils may appreciate a fresh look at material covered earlier in Year 6 especially if they had not quite grasped it the first time round. A second pass through it is sufficient, sometimes, to enable the 'penny to drop'.

Some Year 7 pupils will not have undertaken investigations in Year 6, or perhaps will not have had an opportunity to use practical equipment (ranging from geometry tools to graph paper). For such pupils, Year 7 can present a new challenge which can be used effectively to grab their interest in the early stages of Key Stage 3. On the other hand there may be significant contradictions between the two phases, for example in the use of calculators which, counter to their previous school's policy, may be allowed, restricted or prohibited! It is likely to remain true though, that pupils' most preferred aspects of mathematics will be investigative or practical, including the use of computers and calculators. A close-run second will be the Handling Data attainment target, including charting and other graphical activities. The least liked aspects of Key Stage 3 mathematics, matching its Key Stage 2 precursor, will tend to be the medley of concepts and processes e.g. fractions, decimals, number rules etc. under the Number attainment target.

Continuity and progression in English

Overview of Key Stage 2 to 3 English

One of the most striking dimensions of the design of the National Curriculum is the explicit recognition of 'process-based' work. These process-based attainment targets are usually the first attainment target (AT1) listed for any programme of study and in English it is Speaking and Listening. For many teachers in both phases, the early stages of coming to terms with the new curriculum would have presented some difficulties as they became obliged to give pupils a greater role in their own learning. Others would have recognized the resonance the new requirements had with what they had already been doing:

> People got very uptight about what exactly is Speaking and Listening but we were all doing [it] from the year dot anyway...maybe for some teachers who didn't really emphasize that, it drew it to their attention that it was a very important part of the curriculum.
>
> (Year 6 Teacher)

In Sutherland *et al.*'s study, most of the Key Stage 3 teachers of English considered that the Speaking and Listening AT and the two Reading and Writing ATs were more or less on a par in terms of the incoming pupils' levels of attainment. These targets are very thematic, indeed not just in English but across the curriculum. It might be reasonable then to argue that curriculum continuity is easier to establish in English than perhaps in mathematics or science and the comments of one teacher would be illustrative of such a notion:

> English...can lend itself to continuity...it is very much a recursive subject...dealing with language all of the time...adding to what they already know. Going back and reinforcing what you have done.
>
> (Head of English)

Progression of course will be a different matter. As we discussed earlier, it is a very much an individual pupil issue rather than any constant characteristic of the intake group.

Year 6 pupils' achievements in English on entry to Year 7

Generalizing about the extent of accomplishment, or lack of it, of a class of new Year 7s will always be fraught with difficulty, in English no less than any other subject. Nevertheless, planning for Year 7 must be carried out and the most logical approach is to use information from Year 6 to do it. It is compulsory for primary schools to pass on information but as we shall discuss in the next chapter the assimilation of the information by Key Stage 3 teachers may not be successfully accomplished. It might be because the basic information is inadequate or indeed it might be because the information doesn't work its way through the complexities of the secondary school's communication system to reach the right people, the Year 7 English teachers.

Many Year 7 English teachers can draw on their experience to project likely levels of attainment and knowledge for their expected new batch of pupils. Complaints will often be heard, for example, about the general low level of writing ability of new intake pupils in recent years. Inevitably, of course, there must be some variation in accomplishment within this general picture. This variation arises from individual abilities and the primary school backgrounds the pupils have, but some common themes persist. For example, many Year 7 teachers would argue that there is widespread experience of pupils having difficulty in providing pieces of extended writing. Complaints about weakness in technical aspects of writing are now par for the course, not just in the KS2/3 transition but in every walk of life where the written word is important, with low levels of competence in punctuation, spelling, paragraphing, grammar and proofing being regularly bemoaned. At a higher level, talking about texts probably reaches an acceptable level of accomplishment although some Year 7 teachers would probably still complain:

> I had a chat with my class and they told me...that they didn't compare characters or do character studies...it was more a case of 'What did you think of [the book]?' and 'Would you recommend it to your friends?'
>
> (Head of English)

In contrast, writing about the texts they have read may well also be quite unfamiliar to incoming Year 7s. To some extent this will be understandable if the underlying objective of their Key Stage 2 reading was the perfectly reasonable pursuit of the enjoyment of reading rather than the critique of literature *per se*. In such cases, Year 7 teachers should not be surprised that technical terms such as alliteration, simile and allegory are not familiar to the majority of their new intake!

Speaking and Listening skills may well fair better in terms of Year 7 pupils' accomplishments. The emphasis on oral work, and expressive activities such as drama and discussion, has been enthusiastically endorsed in Key Stage 1 and 2 and most Year 7 teachers should find some resonance with the view:

> The children love drama...they are quite used to moving the furniture around...working in groups...it must come from the primary schools...
>
> (English Teacher)

Deciding how to start Year 7 English

Most English teachers consider Year 7 to be both a fresh start and a follow-on. Much of the first period of induction in a new school therefore involves exploration of the extent of pupils' attainments. Good, imaginative planning of what the pupils will do in this first period in their new school will have a major effect on the pupils' motivation and general settling in. Year 7 English teachers tend to use two main approaches to capture the pupils' interest. The first is to use a special introductory unit designed to acclimatize the pupils gently to the standard and the style of working, and to enable them to get to know each other. The second approach is more conventional but no less effective if carefully planned: beginning new pupils on the Key Stage 3 programme through literature-based work.

Sutherland *et al.* reported that introductory units usually took the theme of 'Early days at School X' or were more personally focused, for example on themes like 'All about me' and so on. It often lasted for the two months up to half-term with perhaps two periods a week given over to it after the initial settling-in period.

> It is called an 'Early Days' project. We felt that in order to make this new world of [school name] meaningful to the children, our starting point should be with them.
>
> (Head of English)

> They do two projects. One is about themselves…and the other is a biography of an older person:…a parent, a grandmother, an elderly relative or just someone they know. This relates to the overall theme for the year of Similarity and Difference…because there is a whole range of activities in talking and listening, reading and writing based on that, we get a very good understanding of them and where they are. On their second project, we do a group project and they work together.
>
> (Head of English)

Through the course of the introductory unit some texts might also be studied, although probably not to the same depth as later texts. Reading or composing poems on the themes of personal development, self-awareness and school-days, with titles such as 'My first day at school' or 'My possessions' etc. can be popular, while discussions on TV soaps such as Byker Grove, Grange Hill etc. can provide useful and relatively widely encountered links with the early teenager culture that the new school presents.

These early days in the Key Stage 2 English classroom will also present many opportunities for a pastoral dimension to the pupils' induction:

> they talk very much about starting at [school name] and their feelings about it…because that gives them the opportunity to express any doubts or fears or hopes and expectations. They keep a diary for the first week…their thoughts and feelings. We do a section on their hopes and ambitions…we talk about their friendship groups…
>
> (Head of English)

The second main approach is to start into the Key Stage 3 programme using a literature unit, based usually on a relatively modern novel. For example:

> *Boy* [Roald Dahl] is a good book to start with because it's a whole school experience. It's about coming into school...I use that at the start, in a pastoral care way as well, so they can talk about how they felt when they first came into [school name]. And they did poems... creative writing about coming into school.
>
> (English Teacher)

Another title which could prove useful in focusing on a new school context for an introductory literature unit is *The Diddakoi* (Rumer Godden). This story features a gypsy child joining a new community and going to school. Other novels which have, at least in part, a 'new school' theme might include *The Friends* (Rosa Guy) and *The Dragon in the Garden* (Reginald Maddock).

Basing all three attainment targets around the novel will enable teachers to assess the extent of the pupils' skills and learning in this exploratory phase. The novel can act as a springboard for many activities including poetry related to the theme, personal impressions and opinions on the issues and so on. This novel-based approach may have some similarity with the frequently used 'project' approach of Key Stage 2 but it is likely that the more in-depth approach to complex concepts such as friendship, loneliness, conflict and so on in the secondary school may be new to the incoming pupils.

Writing is the attainment target most likely to attract the teachers' interest in terms of assessing pupils' capabilities:

> [F]rom the results of that first project plus a written biography...of a person of their own choice...I then have a fairly good idea by the end of October...exactly what sort of English skills they have...
>
> (English Teacher)

In addition to biography, many other styles and genres of writing can be introduced to engage the pupils' interest including autobiography (e.g. the 'All about me' theme), converting a Shakespeare excerpt to the modern spoken word, retelling a story from one of its character's perspectives, scripting trailers for films developed from one of the class novels and so on. These may then be used to assess and develop the various basic skills (including spelling, punctuation and grammar), higher order skills (such as planning, design and argument) and higher order attributes (like creativity and reflectiveness).

Continuity and progression in mathematics

Overview of Key Stage 2 and 3 mathematics

Mathematics teachers work to a tightly bounded and highly specified curriculum and within each type of school, primary and secondary, there is generally a well-developed continuity in the pupils' year-on-year experience of learning. As we have discussed earlier, however, there is a strong likelihood of planned discontinuity in the transition phase. Pupils are likely to experience some form of fresh start, usually based on either a pre-determined level of attainment in a fixed area of the curriculum or a general revision of Key Stage 2-type areas of study in an endeavour to assess the pupils' attainments. The reason for these strategies is that while a continuous curriculum might be in place, strict 'follow-on' continuity would require all of the feeder primary schools to have followed exactly the same programme in more or less the same manner, and all of the pupils to have reached the same level of attainment in the relevant areas. Repetition will probably feature in their early days in Key Stage 3 but this perception may often mask more complex working in the same topics e.g. from working with fractions ('We've done fractions before!') to multiplying fractions – what the pupils might call 'harder' work in the sense that it is likely to be a progression for many of them.

Mathematics is one of the subjects (science is certainly another) in which there will probably also be a degree of discontinuity in the pupils' experience of the learning environment. All Key Stage 3 subjects will of course be offered in a compartmentalized timetable, largely unfamiliar to Year 6 pupils. However there will also be less tangible differences in teaching and learning style and classroom management. Compared to the integrated, thematic approach to mathematics – which many of them would have experienced in Key Stage 2 – Year 7 mathematics will tend to be more regimented. The common experience will be of a series of relatively discrete and brief units designed to build continuously to the end-of-Key Stage 3 tests and to provide a platform for Key Stage 4. They might also find that the freedom of movement that many of them would have enjoyed in their primary classrooms is replaced by a more formal classroom regime.

Year 6 pupils' achievements on entry to Year 7

One area likely to have a wide variety of levels of achievement or indeed exposure, is the process attainment target AT1: Using and Applying Mathematics. Some Year 7 teachers will express the view that it is not addressed properly in Key Stage 2 but the likelihood is that the reason for the diversity and perhaps low levels of attainment among entering Year 7 pupils is that their literacy and recording skills are not up to the task. The competence necessary to follow instructions, record observations and explain what they find may be underdeveloped in some pupils, depending on their experience in primary school, and it might be quite advanced in others:

> They know what they want to say but they can't express themselves on paper...in an intelligible way that I can understand...I always say to them: 'Now your Gran is going to read this and she doesn't know anything about it. Could she understand what you've been doing?'...they agree that she couldn't understand what they have written.
> (Mathematics Teacher)

Clearly ability will have a bearing on the extent to which this type of literacy can be developed but the Key Stage 2 approach to investigative mathematics, to its planning, recording and reporting, may well be the more influential factor.

It is likely that some members of any Year 7 class will have gaps in their mathematics background. Any number of circumstances can give rise to such a situation. For example, the pupils' teacher may have been on sick leave for a time leaving a substitute teacher to try to keep up a coherent programme. Perhaps some of the pupils themselves had been absent on important occasions and the particular set of mathematical experiences therefore eluded them. Their Year 6 teacher may not have felt confident or competent enough in particular topics to spend sufficient time on them with the pupils or maybe they just ran out of time and the topics were omitted.

Clearly this type of situation could hinder achievement in any subject but in mathematics it can be more damaging as the pupils fail to grasp fundamental concepts in, for example, number theory. Often the result is that the pupil struggles with later work because of these shaky foundations. The ATs Shape, Space and Measures and Number will tend to have the least gaps in pupil experience as they are generally the staple topics of Key Stage 2. However there may be significant variation in Number arising from the use, in primary schools, of different methods for common processes, the most notable of these being subtraction. Some degree of variation in levels of attainment can also be expected at the beginning of Year 7 in such areas as fractions, decimals, place value etc. while in Using and Applying Mathematics planning and reporting skills may well be weak with a significant number of incoming pupils.

Deciding how to start Year 7

In schools where there is no banding or streaming, the problem of teaching classes with pupils of varied abilities and attainment levels in mathematics is likely to be most acute. However, even in those schools that do arrange their Year 7 classes in terms of prior achievement, the teachers will still experience sufficient variety in their Year 7 classes to warrant some degree of differentiated teaching. Differentiated approaches to teaching are complex and a number of strategies are adopted. The most usual is to provide extension work for the more able pupils or to build different levels of difficulty into the same topic. A 'partnership' approach is to use groups in which more advanced pupils contribute to the support of weaker classmates. Compounding problems of attainment in the subject, the existence among even a minority of the incoming group of negative perceptions such as fear, confusion and failure in relation to mathematics, can mean an uphill struggle for the Year 7 teacher. Whatever the extent of variation in the group, teachers will not go far wrong if their main objectives for the early days of Year 7 are to motivate the pupils through success and enjoyment.

Within the two main approaches to the start of Year 7 (i.e. starting a standard topic at a pre-determined level of attainment or engaging in a wide-ranging revision of Key Stage 2 mathematics with a view to identifying significant gaps or weaknesses etc.) it is possible to adopt a motivational or even 'novelty' approach. Disguising the mathematics in some enjoyable practical work, such as drawing up flow charts for familiar processes or displaying statistical information on pupils' likes and dislikes in interesting graphics, can be effective in stimulating interest and motivation early on. Novel but unambiguously mathematical topics such as Algebra may also be worthy of adopting in the induction stage but care needs to be taken that the pupils' level of progression matches the conceptual understanding needed for such topics.

Another tack in winning the pupils' interest and commitment is to draw on familiar material:

> I would generally start with number...they are all familiar with it and they need the four rules....table work would be something that I would do at the beginning...making it into sort of a game. We would have a quiz and a bit of a prize, 50p or whatever...
>
> (Mathematics Teacher)

Familiar material, however, obviously holds risks of boredom and disaffection with class work but it can be argued that the very familiarity itself is comforting in the early days of entry to a complex, awe-inspiring institution (which for many pupils is what their new secondary school is).

Repetition can also, of course, be good in its own right. A relatively rapid pass through Number topics, slowing for more in-depth treatment of topics in which some or all of the pupils show inadequate achievement, can reinforce established learning and can help overcome areas of lingering difficulty.

Continuity and progression in science

Overview of Key Stage 2 to 3 science

Aside from the obvious differences in resources and facilities, science is relatively new as a formal subject in most primary schools. This makes it likely that some, perhaps a majority, of the incoming pupils will find science in Year 7 to be a major and hopefully pleasant surprise. However, the old notion of nature study as the primary school's contribution to learning in science has been well-scotched with the development of the National Curriculum. Instead, fundamental areas of science learning, such as those covered by the process attainment target Experimental and Investigative Science, now feature from Key Stage 1 through to the end of Key Stage 2. In addition the work for this AT is often developed within the contexts provided by the other three attainment targets: Life Processes and Living Things, Materials and their Properties, and Physical Processes.

The follow-on to Key Stage 3 is designed to be progressive in terms of increasing complexity of concepts and content and much of the earlier primary years' work is designed to develop familiarity with the processes of scientific enquiry and of the application of science in society. However the perceptions of some Key Stage 3 teachers may well retain a sense of superiority, particularly in viewing science in the primary school as a passive experience (watching teacher demonstrations) and involving a degree of rote learning (e.g. learning parts of the body, the phases of the moon, names of planets etc.):

> We find that primary science tends to be taught as a sort of theory exercise...most of the work seems to have been done as a demonstration to them.
>
> (Head of Science)

As we discussed earlier, this is a perception that may well also be shared by the pupils.

Some Year 7 teachers will recognize the common threads in Key Stage 2 and 3 science but may claim that the inevitably greater potential for investigative and practical science in the secondary school provides a better base for building conceptual understanding:

content wise we're probably trying to get across the same type of content...but in a widely different fashion. We would base it very much on the practical investigative approach, trying to get across some of the key concepts and really building for the future...

(Head of Science)

Key Stage 2 teachers, however, are very much constrained in anything they do in science and although they may be fewer in number as time goes on, their detractors in Key Stage 3 would do well to pause and consider the successes that are won in Key Stage 2 despite the difficulties. Many of their Key Stage 2 colleagues will have had only short-term in-service support for teaching science; they will have very limited resources and facilities, an expectation that they should teach almost every subject that can claim its worth in primary education, and no technician support!

One likely change for some pupils will be the structure of science in some secondary schools. Single award science programmes which begin in Year 7 will present a major change from the primary school science context and will demand special attention from the Year 7 teachers to ensure that it does not add to the pupils' sense of confusion in their early days at the school. Surprisingly perhaps, some of the routine teaching and learning arrangements of the sciences (for example group working and whole class discussions) may well act as comforting processes in the settling-in period.

The issue of repetition in science is often attributed to particular practical exercises, for example chromatography of plant extracts or filtration of aqueous mixtures. When the pupils say 'We've done that before', the Year 7 teachers could be forgiven for harbouring irritation that a particularly important practical activity has had its thunder stolen in the primary school. However it is probably the case that the primary school teacher could not engage in the time and development, and perhaps the pupils' individual 'hands-on' participation, that can be afforded in the secondary school. It is up to the Year 7 teacher, then, to exploit what the pupils already know and to develop it further:

For instance...I would ask what things they had done in school to produce a sound...they would talk about a drum, cymbals and so on and we would discuss that. And then I would introduce some of the technical language they might not have used before; they might just have called it 'hitting a drum makes a sound'. So I would introduce words like 'vibration'...it is a gradual thing but I would make sure that I relate back to what I think they might have learned in the primary school.

(Physics Teacher)

Year 6 pupils' achievements on entry to Year 7

As in mathematics, Year 7 science teachers are likely to complain about entering pupils' levels of literacy and their capacity to plan, record and report work in an investigative context. Practical measurement, human and plant biology, and electrical circuits will probably form a core of common experience among the incoming pupils while at a conceptual understanding level, Year 7 teachers might well concede, even if it is grudgingly in some cases, that the pupils: 'all have a good idea of fair testing...that makes any further development very easy for us...'. The AT with the least attention paid to it in Key Stage 2 is likely to be Materials and their Properties, particularly the chemistry related topics. With the very real difficulties associated with teacher competence in the science ATs and with science resources and facilities generally in the primary school, there is more chance of definable gaps in the pupils' science background work than in mathematics or English.

Deciding how to start Year 7

Almost the first contact with science for new Year 7 pupils will be in the laboratory context and this makes the choice of starting point very simple for most science teachers. Laboratory safety and other general health and safety issues are almost mandatory introductory topics in which rules and routines are set out for the rest of the year. This introductory activity will be virtually universal for all Year 7 pupils but as a rule it doesn't take very long to complete and the question of how the science programme itself will begin will always require answering.

Science teachers in Year 7, perhaps more so than mathematics teachers who can more easily engage in general revision or English teachers who can exploit pupils' personal experiences or imaginations, are likely to set a common, pre-determined topic and level of attainment in it to begin Year 7. The extent of planning, for experiments, materials, equipment etc., means that such a strategy is not just a planned discontinuity, it may well be constrained by physical circumstances. However such an approach is not necessarily restrictive or vulnerable to charges of repetition, indeed it can be made to be relatively novel and motivational for the pupils:

> The last year or so we have moved the kids straight into chemistry. Just setting up apparatus, separation techniques...the use of beakers and funnels and all that, and the idea of safety....Their expectations are very high: 'We want to be doing something that's very "sciencey"!' So we would move into that AT early on. It mightn't be the easiest one,

but it certainly is the one that we would feel gets them off on the right foot in secondary school.

(Head of Science)

Other possible motivation-capturing units might include classification skills of familiar topics, for example types of animals, or familiar topics that enable the pupils to display their existing knowledge and skills, for example in electricity or measurement. Very often, Year 7 teachers will try to extend such familiar and conventional topics by taking an unusual slant, such as examining circuits in battery operated toys that the pupils bring in or by challenging them to make unusual measurements such as the volume of a stone or the thickness of a page. On entering Year 7 and meeting with repetition of work they have done in Key Stage 2, pupils are apt to think or even say: 'I've done that. Why am I doing it again?' Their motivation can be dented and they can even 'switch off' if the teacher does not take care to exploit their prior knowledge and to build upon it.

Summary

This chapter has delved into the detail that teachers in Year 6 and Year 7 must deal with in the transition process. It presents some of the difficulties and dilemmas experienced by the teachers. For example, Year 7 teachers will receive pupils from a number of different schools with potentially wide variation in educational experience and in levels of achievement. Year 6 teachers will often perceive, often correctly, that their hard work in Year 6 is put on hold as the Year 7 teachers strike a low level of class work in response to the variety of levels of accomplishment that their new pupils have. The chapter presents teachers in the core subjects in secondary schools and in Year 6 in primary schools with options and ideas for:

1   preparing Year 6 pupils for Year 7;
2   liaison activities between Year 6 and Year 7 teachers;
3   deciding how to begin Year 7.

Note

1   All quotations in this chapter come from the study *The Transition between Key Stage 2 and Key Stage 3* (1996) by Sutherland, Johnston and Gardner unless otherwise noted.

Chapter 5

Transfer of information

Issues
- Who knows pupils' strengths and weaknesses?
- What information has to be exchanged?
- What other types of information are available?
- Can the information be exchanged in electronic form?
- How should transferred information be used?

This chapter addresses the crucial area of communication between schools and teachers and between schools and parents. School-to-school interaction is based on the exchange of academic and pastoral information on transferring pupils and on the ways in which this can be accomplished using conventional paperwork, liaison visits and meetings, and information technology. School-to-parent interaction has a different set of objectives, including informing them of the school's quality and achievements and reassuring them of a secure environment for their children. The concepts and purposes underlying the processes are discussed in terms of good practice and the roles and responsibilities of teachers on both sides of the transition are explored.

Information on pupils

The key person at the start of the transition process is undoubtedly the Year 6 teacher. Almost all primary classes will have only one teacher in Year 6 and it will be this teacher who guides them through the last year of Key Stage 2, their last year of primary schooling. It is also the Year 6 teacher who, by the end of the year, will know the pupils best in terms of their performance and progression. Any transfer of information or any liaison activities are relatively meaningless if the Year 6 teacher is not involved. Before we develop the whole process, however, it is well to remember that the early days of transition begin some time in Year 5. The Year 5 teachers will often find themselves having to begin the process of acclimatizing their pupils to the prospect of primary school ending. The preparation will probably not be explicit in any particular sense but they will probably have to respond to questions from pupils themselves, and indeed their parents, as they see the cohort ahead of them preparing to leave. The Year 5 teacher must therefore be *au fait* with all matters about 'transition' (e.g. schools, procedures, selection etc. as appropriate) to help explain and perhaps to advise about forthcoming options and processes.

The importance of the information the Year 6 teacher has is unquestionable. Teaching must rest upon assumptions about what children can or cannot do and what development needs they have. These assumptions, if they are to be valid, must therefore draw on relevant sources of information on the pupils' progress. Year 7 teachers cannot fully plan the teaching programme for a new intake unless they have this type of information to guide them. There is an easy way out, of course: simply adopt a 'fresh start' strategy. This approach often assumes nothing about the pupils' level of attainment and starts from a low level e.g. Level 3. As we discuss in Chapter 3, there are good as well as bad reasons for adopting such a course. The Year 7 teacher may simply bow to the fact that the pupils are at various levels of accomplishment and that they have a wide range of experiences, including gaps, in the subject. They decide, therefore, to assume nothing and treat all of the pupils the same. They pick a topic that will fit in with the Key Stage 3 programme and they start it at a predetermined low level so as to have as many pupils moving together on it as possible. One significant alternative to planning in the dark, so to speak, is to use information transferred from the primary schools. The responsibility for developing this information ultimately rests with the Year 6 teacher in the primary school.

Pupils' strengths and weaknesses

Few would argue that Year 6 teachers have an in-depth knowledge of their young pupils. Dealing with them all day every day for a whole year provides for a body of insights and information that cannot, by nature of the very different contexts, be paralleled by teachers in secondary schools. Most Year 6 teachers will know, perhaps without being able to articulate the reasons for knowing, how their pupils develop, how they learn, and how best they can be motivated and encouraged. Having this in-depth knowledge carries certain professional obligations and responsibilities.

In relation to transition, for example, Year 6 teachers have to respond to demands and expectations that emanate from sources outside the school; most notably from parents but also from the secondary schools to which their pupils will be going. They must also have a clear perception and understanding of the knowledge base upon which the National Curriculum is designed, particularly in relation to the three core subjects: English, mathematics and science. Their intimate knowledge of the Key Stage 2 curriculum must be complemented by a thorough awareness of the continuity and progression factors involved in the follow-on defined by the

Key Stage 3 programmes of study. With this grasp of the continuity and progression issues across the transition, Year 6 teachers are well placed to assist Year 7 teachers in their planning. Clearly such an input must depend on there actually being communication and information transfer between the two types of teachers.

Transfer of information

Statutory requirements

It can be argued that all academic and pastoral information relating to a pupil should be transferred to the receiving school. The pastoral information will include positive details on such matters as sports and arts achievements, hobbies and so on. Some will also argue that negative pastoral information (relating for example to attitudes and behaviour) should also be sent, but the ethical issues related to such material do bear consideration before so doing. The simplest and indeed strongest argument against a policy of sending all available details centres on the manageability of such information. Assuming that every one of the receiving Year 7 teachers, and there may be as many as ten or twelve, were interested in the information, the prospect of many pages of a detailed and wide-ranging profile would prove daunting for most teachers. There is also the question of relevance. How relevant would a mathematics profile, going back to Key Stage 1, be to a Year 7 English teacher? Clearly, manageability and relevance are paramount concerns and to date the policy has been to require primary schools to provide a basic minimum of information for secondary school usage.

The statutory requirements for the transfer of information between schools focus on the SAT scores for Key Stage 2 in combination with the Year 6 teacher's 'teacher assessment' scores. These must be passed to the receiving schools in good time for them to plan how they will accommodate the new pupils and should include details of any special considerations that may be necessary. Timing will probably prove a problem, however, unless schools agree dates between themselves. Neither SCAA nor the DfEE prescribe the deadlines, preferring local arrangements to be made – perhaps a subtle way of ensuring that schools talk to each other.

Since July 1997, primary schools have had additional information from the end-of-Key Stage tests to pass on to their secondary colleagues. This additional information comprises:

- actual test scores (and the level thresholds for the tests);
- age-standardized scores for reading, spelling, mathematics and mental arithmetic;
- separate levels from the tests for reading and writing;

- separate teacher assessment levels for each attainment target.

The provision of the actual test scores in each subject area is designed to enable schools to compare the pupil's performance with the threshold score that is used for allocating the level they have been awarded. For example, a score of 26 would be interpreted as a marginal performance at Level 4 if the threshold score for allocating a Level 4 was 25. The provision of the actual score and the threshold score for the level therefore helps to give meaning to terms such as 'She's a solid Level 4' or 'He's a weak Level 5'. The age-standardized scores are designed to be additionally helpful by allowing comparison between the pupil's actual score in the test (reading, mathematics etc.) and the standardized score for the whole population of pupils with the same birthday month as the pupil in question. SCAA (1997: 4) propose a diagnostic use for this type of information, albeit with a caution on reading too much into the comparison of a raw test score against the standardized score range. They suggest that the information can 'be useful in a variety of ways, for example to:

- give a profile of the range of ability in a group;
- compare this profile with a national profile, based on a "normal" distribution;
- help identify pupils with special educational needs and those with exceptional ability; and
- help identify older pupils who may be underperforming, or younger pupils who may be performing very well in relation to their age.'

Primary schools are also sent guidance from SCAA on how to identify separate reading and writing levels from the English test results. This facility is designed to assist schools in applying the tests more diagnostically by providing information on the relative strengths and weaknesses in these two areas of the English programme of study. Clearly such information would be very useful to Year 7 English teachers and, in order to raise their awareness, SCAA sends Key Stage 3 schools copies of the tests for all three subjects and information on the level thresholds and age-standardized scores.

At the end of Key Stage 2, teachers are required to make judgements ('teacher assessments') about the level of attainment reached by each pupil in the core subjects. Although the discrete attainment target levels are then combined to produce an overall subject level for reporting to parents, the separate results provide a picture of the pupil's progress. Again these results represent information that will probably be important for teachers in Year 7.

Neither SCAA nor the DfEE prescribe whether any or all of the additional information must be transferred but they do strongly encourage its transfer. In the pamphlet *Making Effective Use of Key Stage 2 Assessments* (SCAA 1997), the example of a possible transfer form includes all of the details mentioned above with additional comments on attendance, attitude to work and behaviour. There is also reference, if appropriate to the particular child, to special educational needs, including individual education plans, to the stage of English language acquisition and to registration on the Child Protection Register. The last part of the form indicates whether additional information (such as the most recent annual report to parents or the end-of-Key Stage 1 assessments) is also enclosed. The annual report to parents represents a particularly valuable source of information for secondary schools as it should provide information on all of the subjects the pupil has studied in Key Stage 2. SCAA (1997: 10) consider it likely that these reports would 'contain the following information about each subjects taught in the primary school:

- the understanding pupils have of key aspects of a subject;
- the extent to which pupils have developed subject-specific skills; and
- the range of strengths and weaknesses pupils bring to a subject.'

To make the most effective use of all of these materials, indeed to ensure that the material is going to be welcomed and used, teachers from both Key Stages need to meet and agree the content of the information transfer. The only way that a Year 6 teacher, or the primary school principal, can know if the information they are transferring is what their secondary school colleagues want, is to meet with them and discuss it!

Types of information

Year 6 teachers will generally have two types of information: academic and pastoral. In either case, the teacher's information may be relatively factual and objective (e.g. 'needs to wear glasses to see the board' or 'has been awarded a Level 4 in the end-of-Key Stage 2 English test') or it may be judgemental (e.g. 'is truculent and sulky' or 'will excel in mathematics'). Factual information needs to be both accurate and up-to-date but will often include a profile of performance measures that give insights into the pupil's progress over a period of time leading up to Year 6. For example the Year 6 teacher will have the end-of-Key Stage SAT scores, including details of attainment target scores for each of the three assessed subjects: English, mathematics and science. In combination with the more judgemental 'teacher assessment' levels for the process-based attainment targets e.g. Speaking and Listening, this represents the most up-to-date assessment of the pupils. However, there is likely to be a wealth of information that can also be used to profile the pupil's progress since entering the school. In many cases, Year 6 teachers will have access to the pupils' end-of-Key

Stage 1 teacher assessments and SAT scores. They may also be able to refer to portfolios of the pupils' work in Key Stage 1 and Key Stage 2, reports to parents, notes of annual and *ad hoc* parent–teacher meetings and a wide variety of standardized literacy and numeracy tests conducted throughout the preceding years. In some cases there may also be statements of special educational needs and individual education plans (IEPs).

Such personal records and other sensitive pastoral records may give rise to ethical concerns in relation to their more judgemental aspects. For example, when such information refers to complex issues such as perceived domestic circumstances or personal attributes, it needs to be treated with great care as it can lead to pre-judgement of a pupil's worth and progress, perhaps to the detriment of the pupil concerned.

A great deal is expected from the Key Stage 2 teacher in terms of assessment, recording and the transfer of relevant, coherent and practical information. How can such a task be made more manageable? Planning for the various assessments is the key. Knowing what you are going to do, and when you are going to do it, is paramount to being successful while having a recording system that is manageable and accessible is vital. Such issues are clearly whole school issues, but Year 6 teachers can make life easier for themselves if they consider the following when planning their assessments (adapted from SCAA 1997).

Long-term targets

The end of Year 6 assessments should concentrate on pupils' attainments using the level descriptions. The evidence collected should include end-of-Key Stage 2 teacher assessments and test outcomes in the core subjects.

Medium-term targets

These should be half termly or at least termly, with the focus being on the medium-term learning objectives for a class. The evidence that needs to be collected should include examples that illustrate progress in pupils' work. These should be added to their records or profiles and over the year there should be sufficient breadth in the examples to cover attainment in all the subject areas of learning.

Short-term targets

These should be daily or perhaps weekly notes, systematically logged, about children needing further support in particular areas or their successes in more challenging work.

Identifying specific learning objectives and recording their outcome in a systematic way will allow reliable judgements to be made about individual pupils, which can then be transferred in an accessible and logical way.

Electronic transfer of information

Information and communications technology (ICT) presents the best possibility in recent times for the ease of transfer of accessible information on pupils' progress and other achievements. Several aspects of the schools' information technology developments are converging rapidly and will provide the technical underpinning for a virtual revolution in information dissemination and exchange. These are:

- the launch of the National Grid for Learning (NGfL);
- the favourable pricing policies for schools that are being adopted by telecommunications agencies;
- the continuing and rapid development of electronic mail (e-mail), the Internet and the World Wide Web;
- the increasing sophistication, while retaining ease of use, of commercially produced administration systems for schools; and
- the requirement that all teachers, by the year 2000, be competent users of ICT.

The level of computing power, which is now available to schools at a relatively modest cost, means that many secondary schools have computer suites that are the envy of the commercial sector. Primary schools lag somewhat behind in terms of the volume of hardware but they are just as sophisticated in their multimedia and Internet needs as any secondary school. As time goes on, the benefits of administrative computing will probably be appreciated by growing numbers of schools. Indeed all schools in Northern Ireland, bar the very smallest of rural schools, have already fully computerized their administrative systems, not just in the obvious areas such as purchasing and salaries but also the complex functions of timetabling, staff cover and daily rolls, and most importantly in pupil records, value-added analyses and curriculum analysis.

One additional development is ultimately likely to have a major impact on the consolidation of ICT solutions to schools' information exchange: the Unique Pupil Number which every person in the future and every person currently being educated will have (DfEE 1997). This number will eventually enable authorized users to access the educational record of any pupil through central and local database record systems. The proposed Common Pupil Record will contain all of the standard details including those suggested by QCA for the 'transfer form' and additional details such as the period of attendance at a particular school, Key Stage 1 baseline assessment records and courses of study taken by post-16 students.

The benefits of an ICT solution to information transfer may well depend on the form of the information transfer. The simplest form is the ubiquitous fax machine. This has the benefit of arriving in paper form although this paper is often the flimsy thermal paper of basic fax machines. Faxes delivered through a computer's fax facility may have the slight advantage of enabling better printed copies. However there are several problems with a simple fax solution. The first is that the document is not a 'live' file. As a print-out, it comes in one piece and any selectivity by the receiver must be carried out using scissors and photocopying! Again with a simple fax, sending information to more than one location at a time can be cumbersome and expensive. Some of these problems are resolved when using e-mail.

The transfer of information by e-mail can be either in the form of a message or as a document 'attached' to a message. In the former case the message can be placed directly into a wordprocessor as a 'live' file that can be worked upon, perhaps to divide up for different people (e.g. head of Year 7 English, head of Year 7 mathematics etc.). One drawback of the simple e-mail message approach is that it quickly reaches a limit on the size of the message it can transmit and receive. The latter case of attaching a file resolves this problem by enabling substantial documents to be sent as additional files. These documents are already in a 'live' wordprocessor file format i.e. they can be worked on immediately without any further manipulation. E-mail also has the advantage of enabling the creation of a distribution group e.g. with all of the target schools' e-mail addresses conveniently under one name (as a more sophisticated fax machine might also allow). The sender simply creates the message and any attached files and sends them at the click of the *Send* or other appropriate button.

For the receiving school, the use of file formats which provide the information in a form ready for assimilation by the school's own computerized administration system is perhaps the ultimate in information transfer. Once into the receiving school, pre-set procedures can enable the computer to collate the appropriate pieces of information for the relevant people i.e. end-of-Key Stage 2 English records for the Year 7 teachers, pastoral information for the year head or induction tutor, and so on. For such an exchange to happen in the first place, however, it is clearly imperative that both schools have the same or wholly compatible administration systems. The transmitting school will of course also find advantages in setting up automated reporting systems which at the click of a button will draw the necessary information, in the required format, from the school's record system and automatically send it on to the requesting or targeted receiving school.

The hardware and software necessary to sustain these various forms of transfer are now commonly, and increasingly cheaply, available. Two hidden but perhaps more important developments are increasingly underpinning progress in these matters. The first is that the underlying tariff system for the use of telephone lines or cables is becoming more affordable for schools and is being backed heavily by a sympathetic government. The second is the rapid improvement that is being made in the technical infrastructure of cable, telephone and digital broadcast systems. This nationwide improvement is being supported through government initiatives such as the National Grid for Learning and through major investment by the telecommunications industry. As will be mentioned later, the potential for audio-visual communications is also beginning to be exploited by many institutions through, for example, video-conferencing.

The use of transfer information

Perhaps unsurprisingly, research such as that of Wynne Harlen (1995) would suggest that the information transferred from primary to secondary schools is largely an 'underused resource'. Yet few would argue that a primary concern of Year 7 teachers and coordinators is to have information on the new intake of pupils that is comprehensive, accurate and accessible, and which will enable good planning for their Year 7 programme. The assessment of children's progress plays a crucial role in teachers' decisions about what work needs to be covered or re-taught. It is very important for Year 7 teachers to know what pupils have been taught previously and how much they have or have not achieved. Some Year 7 teachers may also find it useful to receive examples of work from Year 6 pupils while information on schemes of work will greatly assist the maintenance of continuity and progress.

For teachers attempting to match the challenge of the Year 7 work to the levels of attainment achieved by the incoming pupils, the Key Stage 2 schemes of work in their subject area may well be an essential addition to the level scores themselves. Schemes of work that provide information about the nature and level of work undertaken will be particularly valuable. In English they might detail the books read and the types of creative writing contexts used, while in mathematics the levels of attainment in Number and the other attainment targets might be exemplified. In science, important information about investigations and experiments undertaken may enable the Year 7 science teacher to begin with a topic or experiment that is completely new. The better the information on the scheme of work followed in whatever subject, the better able the relevant Year 7 teachers will be to dovetail their own programmes to build on the Year 6 work.

At the school level, information which is not up-to-date or is simply incorrect can give rise to mistakes being made when the receiving school is deciding its class groupings. Mistakes might most commonly be made in streaming or setting, owing perhaps to incorrect or otherwise insufficient information on levels of attainment, but sometimes because the end of Year 6 tests are simply not available in time for the secondary schools to decide on their groups. It is not unusual for the secondary schools to get around this problem by asking the primary schools directly for 'teacher assessment' information.

Mistakes or omissions in pastoral records are just as conceivable. For example, if there is a history of difficulty between two pupils and the primary school neglects to mention it, the problem could arise again in secondary school and run well into Key Stage 3 before it is noticed. Even if the primary school does identify the problem, and goes as far as to suggest that they be separated in future class groups, it is entirely possible that the information does not get to the relevant coordinator or induction teacher. It is also possible that it gets to the right person but the volume of transferred material conspires to hide these important details.

Year 6 teachers' knowledge of continuity in the core subjects

Clearly there is an onus on the Year 6 teachers to ensure that they know sufficient about each subject to understand how the curriculum proposes to facilitate continuity and progression. In most subjects there are three broad areas to consider:

- progression viewed as the pupils' conceptual development in the subject e.g. logic, understanding, knowledge and ideas;
- progression viewed as developing competence in relevant processes e.g. investigation in science, problem solving in mathematics and creative expression in English;
- progression viewed as increasing assimilation of the content of learning e.g. principles in science, rules of number in mathematics and styles of writing in English.

When planning for progression it is important to identify the best ways of organizing the sequence of experiences to which the children will be exposed. Best practice dictates that there should be progression across the transition and that there should be agreement between primary and secondary schools on the content covered by the pupils in Year 6 and 7.

Summary

This chapter considers the nature and extent of information transfer that is needed between schools. The statutory requirements are discussed and the options for other desirable types of information are considered. The prospects for electronic transfer and the potential this has for widening access to a greater number of appropriate teachers is also addressed. In developing an information transfer policy, schools need to agree on:

1   what information should be transferred and how this transfer should be accomplished;
2   a timetable for transfer of the information;
3   who should manage the delivery, receipt and dissemination of the information in each institution;
4   how to monitor and report upon the effectiveness of the transfer of information.

Chapter 6

Liaison between schools, teachers and parents

Issues
- What should liaison set out to achieve?
- How should liaison be organized?

This chapter addresses the vital issue of cross-phase liaison. Liaison requires cooperation on shared goals with clear objectives. This can only be achieved through targeted organization and collaboration between schools, teachers and parents. The concepts are discussed in terms of good practice and the roles of individuals and institutions are examined. Suggestions are given for ways of enhancing effective practice.

Liaison

A major aspect of improving transition processes is the quality of interaction (i.e. liaison) between the phases and between the schools and the parents and pupils who are 'in transition'. Liaison implies a degree of cooperation on shared goals; in this case the smooth transition of children from one school system at Key Stage 2 to another at Key Stage 3. It also implies face-to-face interaction and not simply correspondence between institutions and people. Schools wishing to initiate or upgrade their liaison with partner schools, parents and pupils will find it useful to consider the following objectives and steps for realizing a successful liaison process.

The objectives for a liaison relationship between primary schools and their destination secondary schools include ensuring that:

- pupils and parents are informed about the options they have;
- there is a smooth transition for the leaving/incoming pupils.

The steps needed to ensure that a successful liaison process is established include:

- deciding how the objectives above will be met;
- identifying the resources needed;

- selecting a suitable liaison person;
- implementing a programme that meets the needs of the pupils, their parents and the partner schools.

Objectives for liaison

The most important focus for the liaison process is the pupils, and with them their parents. Within the cohort of transferring pupils, there will be many who are the oldest children in their families i.e. their parents are facing transition for the first time. It is a worrying time for parents, indeed maybe even more so for them than for their children as very often their apprehension about the impending changes begins much sooner in the Year 5/Year 6 period than that of their children. Wise parents do not let any apprehension they may feel become apparent to their children but the subject of transfer has to be broached nevertheless. Parents that have older children, who have already gone through the transition in earlier years, will also be unlikely to escape some degree of anxiety as the decision, which influences the education of their children during their crucial adolescent years, can rarely be taken lightly.

The task for schools, then, is to recognize the importance of the decisions being made and the apprehension to which they can give rise; factors that are not always obvious to teachers who are comfortably focused on their annual cycle of teaching and who do not necessarily see a need to make special provision for potential newcomers. Clearly there must be effective dissemination of information to potential parents and their children but it must be more than a welcoming letter or a school brochure. Variations on the theme of open days are powerful ways of bringing prospective parents and their children into the school and these will be discussed in more detail below.

When a school elects to engage in a liaison process, it is essentially saying: we want to ensure that there is a smooth and informed transition process for our leaving or incoming pupils. While a change in school will inevitably involve changes in the social, physical and academic contexts in which children will find themselves, 'smooth'-ness nevertheless implies that these changes will be made without any major shocks. Achieving smoothness will therefore require determined planning and action by the liaison teachers on both sides of the transition. Pre-transfer visits will, for example, help to lessen the potential trepidation pupils might experience in preparing for their full-time entry to their new school. Such visits give them a taste of the school's physical characteristics, such as its size and location and its ambience, including the potentially unfamiliar bustle and noise. Opportunities to see teaching in action will also help to acclimatize the new recruits to the probably very different teaching and learning styles, while giving some early exposure to the new set of teachers they will meet.

Smoothness also implies continuity in the curriculum that new pupils will experience, and particularly in the core subjects (mathematics, science and English) which span the transition. These latter issues of curriculum continuity and progression have been examined in Chapter 3 but the professional liaison processes needed to ensure as seamless as possible a transition will also be discussed below.

Meeting the objectives of liaison effectively

In planning how to meet the objectives of a liaison programme, schools on both sides of the divide must ensure they have the necessary resources. In the main these will centre on identifying the right members of staff and enabling them to have the time to undertake the planning and action that will be needed. While it may be possible to absorb these costs in the normal salary bill of both primary and secondary schools, the latter will probably attract additional costs for the development and reproduction of a school brochure, for mailshots and for special events.

Aside from resource considerations, planning to meet the objectives of a liaison programme effectively will tend to focus on the three interfaces:

- with the transferring cohort of pupils;
- with the pupils' parents;
- with colleagues in partner schools (professional liaison).

These are discussed in turn below.

Liaison with pupils

Primary schools and their leaving pupils

Pupils entering their final year in the primary school will become increasingly concerned about the major change ahead of them. They will have a variety of questions, perhaps somewhat naïve to begin with but as time goes on they will become more detailed and sophisticated. Research shows that there is a significant myth culture among the leaving group in a primary school, fuelled to a large extent by ex-pupils in their first year of secondary schooling. Some of these myths carry an element of truth, relating perhaps to such aspects as the amount of homework that will be given in the new schools, but others may well be over-elaborations and exaggerations of the regular 'horror' stories such as frightening initiation ceremonies, bullying by older pupils and nasty teachers. A key element of all of these, regardless of any basis of truth, is the potential to cause anxiety and even fear. Alongside such emotions of course, there will be the more positive senses of excitement and challenge, and the children's own appreciation that they are taking another major step in their growing up.

Clearly it is incumbent on Year 6 teachers to scotch the less savoury rumours and to ease any rising concerns as best they can. More than this, though, they should also be aiming to acclimatize the children to their future school context as best they can. This will normally involve, as a minimum, having up-to-date information on the schools that are on offer to the pupils. Usually in the form of a colourful and illustrated brochure, perhaps even a short video presentation of life in a secondary school (or in the pupils' prospective schools), such materials will provide a first source of information on potential school choices. Better still, however, will be opportunities to hear from visiting teachers talking about their schools and visits to the secondary schools during open days, fêtes, sports events and normal school days. Exposure to teaching in the secondary schools (either in the primary school from visiting teachers or in the secondary schools during pupils' visits to them) is another popular approach that can give the pupils a very real taste of what secondary education holds for them.

Secondary schools and prospective pupils

Secondary schools are now very much in the business of attracting new pupils rather than simply receiving them. The importance of keeping up rolls is well appreciated throughout the sector as staffing and other resourcing-related matters have come to depend so much on enrolled numbers. In areas where there are several secondary schools competing for new pupils, the schools will be keenly aware of the need to project a positive image to prospective pupils. Indeed, they will wish to get to the feeder primary schools early in Year 6 to ensure that the leaving pupils have their school high in the list of possible secondary school choices.

Apart from visits to primary schools, to talk to Year 6 classes etc., more and more secondary schools are organizing joint activities with feeder primaries. At the school level, these can be as varied as joint dramatic productions, sports galas, science fairs and field trips but very innovative joint activities are also happening at the level of teachers working together in each other's schools. Such activities include jointly taught lessons in which primary and secondary pupils cooperate on projects or the mentoring, by the older pupils, of visiting primary pupils in various learning activities including poetry or investigative mathematics.

Secondary schools and their incoming pupils

Once pupils have elected to join a school (or have been selected in a competitive system) the receiving schools need to consider an induction programme to smooth the transition from the familiarity of their primary schools to the potentially awesome and largely unfamiliar world of the secondary school. A crucial measure is to ensure that someone is charged with the responsibility of monitoring and supporting the pupils closely in their first few days in the school, with a facility for continued support (of reducing intensity as the settling-in process takes hold). Other measures, which provide a basis for a smooth induction, will include days in school for the new recruits only. These days may take an activity programme in sport or drama as their theme and are usually designed to help the new pupils to get to know each other and to experience the facilities of the school in a more social context. Sometimes these pre-beginning-of-term days will be some weeks before the start of the new school year, while in other cases the school intake days may be staggered to bring in the first years on their own or perhaps along with the top-age pupils, who then assist in the familiarization process.

Getting induction right may be crucial to the eventual success of the children in secondary education. It is a widely experienced phenomenon that for some children the first couple of years in secondary school result in falling levels of achievement. Many such pupils recover and go on to do well but others continue to slip and may even end up totally disaffected, troublesome and grossly underachieving. The reasons for this type of performance slippage are not clear but two possibilities cannot be ruled out. The first is bad induction. Perhaps over-high expectations for an exciting new phase of life are dampened by the reality of many apparently less interested teachers, seen only a few times a week for a short time on each occasion and then with no personal recognition, just a member of another big class. Maybe the first few weeks are so confusing and even frightening, lost within a sea of strangers and overburdened with unfamiliar and difficult work, that withdrawal is a reasonable coping strategy. Worse, perhaps, will be conditions that allow bullying and intimidation of incoming pupils. Although for most children the apprehension and unfamiliarity lasts for only a short time, it is nevertheless possible that bad induction experiences can lead to relatively permanent disaffection and underachievement.

The second possibility is poor continuity and progression. Children coming into a secondary school are leaving six years of education which for the most part changed in content and increased in challenge as time went on. If they then come into a situation where teachers, either for expediency or simply because they have no information on which to base any other strategy, choose to go for a low-level 'fresh start', problems may well arise. A strategy that inherently drags them back to work they have already mastered, to books and experiments that they have already covered, to a lack of challenge owing to the level at which it is pitched, may well cause regression in learning which may or may not be recoverable as Key Stage 3 eventually climbs away from Key Stage 2 working levels.

Whatever the reason for learning regression in the early secondary years, there is clearly no room for complacency about a strong and effective induction programme.

Liaison with parents

The information to be provided for parents, especially first-time parents with no previous experience of the transfer process, needs to be very focused and produced to a professional standard. The secondary schools themselves will clearly be the source of these materials but often the first dissemination point is in the primary school.

Primary schools and 'transition' parents

Primary schools, and particularly their Year 6 teachers, will often be the first port of call for parents beginning to plan the next stage of their children's education. In areas where a choice is available they will be asking about the quality of the local schools. Their general concerns will focus on whether the schools have a good reputation for discipline, academic attainment, sports and the arts. More specifically they will want to be assured that the schools available to them will provide a secure location for their children, treating them as individuals according to their needs and free from the frightening scourges of substance abuse and bullying, and the worst effects of ill-discipline. The primary school cannot give assurances in any absolute fashion but they will tend to know the reputation and quality of local secondary schools in a more objective way than community hearsay might portray them.

The academic standing of the local schools is probably the easiest criterion to address as information will already be in the public domain from several sources. Of dubious value though they may be, league tables and published inspection reports will provide a set of indicators from which parents may draw some inference. Possibly more valid information, however, will be available from many schools in the form of brochures that set out the school in the round. These brochures often carry interesting articles on the school's history, its successful ex-pupils, its current extra-curricular, artistic, musical and sports achievements and so on. They have the potential to provide a much more welcoming insight into the type of environment the schools will offer for new pupils than the more bland GCSE and A-level performance summaries offered by league tables of various kinds.

Aside from providing documentation, primary schools will find it difficult not to offer more participative activities for parents interested in being informed about transition. These most commonly take the form of information evenings in which the principal and liaison teacher, for example, provide a presentation on the key elements of the transition process. Representatives from prospective secondary schools will often also attend these meetings to provide first-hand responses to parents' concerns and questions. Of course, anyone who has ever attended a school's annual general meeting will know that in any such meeting it is a vociferous few who inevitably ask the questions and get the answers. The more reserved parents, perhaps the majority, will benefit from the answers also, but inevitably some questions will remain unasked. To counteract this, and also to emphasize their 'personal touch', many primary schools will also organize individual meetings between the principal or liaison teacher, as appropriate, and the parents of their leaving pupils. These give all of the parents the opportunity to voice their concerns or seek further information.

Secondary schools and 'transition' parents

In recent years many secondary schools have become adept at selling themselves, some even offering free gifts to parents and pupils who attend open days or to those who select them for enrolment. Such 'gimmicks' may well have some value in cases where there are falling rolls with direct competition between several schools for a relatively small number of pupils. For the most part, however, prospective parents will prefer to be convinced about the qualities of the schools in the terms mentioned above (i.e. academic performance, discipline, sport and the arts); and will also wish to be assured that substance abuse and bullying are not experienced or tolerated. Schools cannot be complacent about these things, even if they are entirely free of them, because the 'tabloid' view of today's schools would have parents believe that secondary schools are tough, ill-disciplined places rife with delinquent problems. Reassuring and welcoming words, strong school-policy outlines and short reports of pupils' achievements, the school's history and annual events, all interspersed with decent pictures of smiling happy children and staff, are the baseline ingredients for effective school brochures and all schools should appreciate the power of such a direct public relations vehicle. Exaggeration should of course be avoided as expectations which are not met can be very damaging in comparison to expectations of a lower order that are met successfully.

In contrast to the primary school's programme for parents of leaving pupils, where the basic objective is to inform parents of the options and the range and features of the secondary schools that are available, the secondary school's programme is deliberately more partial. Here the intention is to persuade the pupils (and their parents) that they should come to that school. The same methods are used however: primarily open days and/or evenings supported by on-request individual meetings with prospective parents.

Open days and evenings are usually very slick operations with the whole staff and many volunteer pupils helping to sell the best points of the school to visiting groups of pupils and their parents. Every part of the school is utilized. The science rooms are abuzz with eye-catching experiments, the art-rooms are festooned with pupils' work, the home economics room ovens are turning out pizza nibbles as fast as the visitors can eat them and the music rooms resound to variations of popular and classical music. The parents revel in the awe they see in their children's eyes while the helpful advice from the attending teachers, sprinkled with reassuring jokes and pleasant small talk, combine to give the air of a well-rounded and friendly environment. A genuine fear shared by many parents is that the familial atmosphere of most primary schools will give way to the unfriendly and unfeeling picture of secondary schooling that is often portrayed in the media. The headteacher's talk to parents should therefore seek to reassure about standards of behaviour and achievement and should be presented in a friendly and welcoming way, rather than in a stern or, worse, an arrogant or dismissive manner.

Professional liaison

Liaison between schools is at the very base of ensuring smooth transitions but very often, even when schools get their liaison with parents and pupils right, there is next to no formal and purposeful liaison between schools. Many schools will of course utilize opportunities for secondary personnel to visit and talk to primary school Year 6s but even in these schools this might be where the liaison ends. Often there is no liaison on the transfer-ring pupils' strengths and weaknesses (other than what is noted in the transfer reports, which primary schools are required to forward to secondary schools), no liaison on special needs, no liaison on pupils' social preferences (e.g. names of close friends who are transferring to the same school) and most importantly no liaison on the pupils' levels of achieve-ment and topics covered in the various subjects.

There may be many reasons for such a situation but prime among them is the likely perception held by Year 6 teachers that even when the information is provided, it is not used by the Year 7 teachers. Anne Sutherland and her colleagues (1996) have shown that Year 7 teachers may not so much be dismissing the primary school information, although an element of this professional arrogance is often apparent, rather they may opt for a fresh start with their new pupils. This strategy is seen as the most expedient in circumstances where the class before them presents as many educational backgrounds as there are feeder schools and as many unfamiliar levels of achievement and understanding as there are pupils.

The official transfer report will list levels of achievement in the core areas but the intimate knowledge of pupils' abilities and achievements has to be developed and will never be effectively transferred in paper (or indeed electronic) form. Nevertheless, effective liaison on pupils' performance in the primary school, particularly Year 6, cannot do other than improve the Year 7 teacher's understanding of his or her new intake's achievements and educational background. There are at least two main ways of accomplishing this goal of effective professional liaison on curriculum continuity and progression.

As outlined in the earlier part of this chapter, the first is to provide the secondary school with documentary evidence of the pupils' achievements. Usually this will mean augmenting the transfer form with a portfolio of pupil work, including a 'record of achievement'-style pupil statement. Clearly this approach has inherent manageability problems. For the primary schools there is the problem of collating the material, and perhaps keeping copies of some of it. However, for the secondary schools the problems loom larger as the number of teachers with a potential need to see evidence of the level of a pupil's work can be as many as 10 per pupil. In practice any portfolio would need to be broken up into relevant topics or subject areas and given to the relevant Year 7 teachers. The alternative, circulating typically 30 complete portfolio folders to each class teacher of each subject, would take weeks to complete and in the meantime the teachers waiting in the queue would still have to use their own resources to build a picture of their new pupils' levels of achievement.

A partial answer to the problem of disseminating information to those who need it most or those to whom it is most relevant, is to send limited information in an easily copyable form. This will mean that it is quick and easy to digest; not much more than the statutory transfer form itself in fact. The receiving school can then decide who should receive it and can pass it directly to them. The near future, however, holds a unique and powerful solution. With the information of the portfolio in electronic form it can be accessed by the relevant teachers to the extent that is relevant to them and when it suits them to access it. This will require the class teachers to have easy access to a computer to enable them to view the material at their convenience. So long as it is structured in a sensible fashion, simple browsing facilities will enable the teachers to find what they want quickly. Clearly any particularly sensitive material, not deemed relevant to the class teachers, would remain accessible only to those like the principal, senior staff etc. who have the necessary access privileges for the system.

Documentary liaison, or simple information transfer, is only of limited benefit. What is probably much more important in terms of curriculum continuity and enabling progression for each pupil without any unnecessary overlap or under-challenge, is professional person-to-person liaison.

We have said several times earlier in the text that Year 6 teachers should have a good awareness of the Year 7 teaching their pupils will receive in their next school and the Year 7 teachers must know the teaching and learning context from which the new entrants have come. There are of course very practical reasons for the Year 7 teachers knowing exactly what has been covered in Year 6. For example the Year 7 science teacher will be able to exploit opportunities for completely new topics, which the pupils have not experienced, if the Year 6 science programme is known in detail through close liaison with the Year 6 teacher. From the opposite perspective, if the Year 6 teachers have an opportunity to observe or team teach in Year 7, they can tailor the approach to their own teaching in Year 6, thereby promoting a degree of continuity in teaching methods. In the English classroom, knowing the literature base that the pupils have is a vital piece of intelligence as the Year 7 teacher plans to develop the first year's reading programme. This information could be provided in paper form but person-to-person interaction will reveal the depth of study and will give insights into how particular pupils have fared in various aspects of the work.

Needless to say, the greater the number of feeder schools represented in the Year 7 class the less chance there is of the Year 7 teacher being able to interact in any realistic way at an individual level with the Year 6 teachers. Schools can and do get around this very practical problem by organizing cluster groups which meet towards the end of each school year or early in the beginning of the incoming year. These groups generally comprise the Year 6 teachers (and occasionally the primary school liaison teachers, if these are different, or the principals) of the feeder schools. They visit as guests of the Year 7 teachers with a view to exchanging experiences and information on the transferring pupils. This formal liaison is often augmented with informal links maintained by telephone and e-mail and by observation visits to each other's schools and classes. Here again, access to sophisticated audio-visual communications is now well within the financial and technical grasp of schools and the near future will begin to see more 'conferencing' between teachers – with audio and video connections through standard desktop computers – on curricular and other matters. This next stage of ICT will obviate the need for teachers to travel to meetings and will greatly facilitate the informal and *ad hoc* communications that are a feature of internal communications between teachers in the same school.

Effective progression in any subject can only be achieved when teachers are in agreement about the levels of assimilation of the underlying concepts, skills and learning that are required by pupils. Collaboration between Year 6 and Year 7 teachers in planning schemes of work and sharing ideas will lead directly to better understanding of each other's domain and indirectly to an enhancement of the learning experience of pupils. For this collaboration to grow, for standards to be shared, much more professional liaison than is currently going on will be needed. Any form of person-to-person interaction, whether by ICT or in cluster meetings, will therefore be a vital step in the process.

The goals of professional liaison

Once communication is established, by conventional or electronic means, teachers on both sides of the transition will find the following guidelines helpful in making the most of the liaison. Year 6 and 7 teachers, who exchange pupils during transition, should:

- agree the content of Year 6 and 7 collaboratively;
- plan the Year 6 and 7 programmes of study jointly;
- have knowledge of what happens in each other's lessons so that a common understanding on what each attainment level represents can develop;
- have a common understanding of the cognitive skills needed for progress to take place in their subject during the transition years;
- agree on what information should be transferred;
- aim to develop understanding of each other's teaching and curriculum programme by viewing each other's practice.

Choosing the liaison teacher

A crucial decision for a school organizing its liaison processes will be the choice of liaison teacher. Several considerations should guide this choice and these are described below. However, it is worth stressing at the outset that liaison with outside bodies and people will be unlikely to be very successful if internal liaison within the school itself is ineffective or, worse still, non-existent. Before identifying a liaison person, then, it is certainly worthwhile for a school to review its own liaison processes; if these are not up to scratch their improvement should proceed in parallel with external liaison developments.

Interpersonal skills top the list of needs for a good liaison person. They will need to make a positive impact with their colleagues in the partner institutions in order to promote successful exchange of ideas and full cooperation on joint ventures. Diplomacy will rank high in the list of necessary skills as there are different sensitivities in different schools and the liaison people must be aware of them. In general, for example, a secondary liaison person who does not empathize with the level of responsibility and variety of duties and teaching that a Year 6 teacher must undertake will not be particularly successful in winning over their primary colleagues. Similarly, primary liaison teachers need to have a good grasp of the complexity facing a Year 7 teacher whose batch of new recruits might come from as many as ten or even more feeder schools with as many different teaching/learning backgrounds as schools. The task of becoming familiar with the new pupils' individual levels of achievement, and their strengths and weaknesses, should not be underestimated by a primary liaison teacher who, in contrast, has in-depth knowledge of the pupils they are sending on.

Another probably important attribute of the successful liaison teacher is enthusiasm. The chances that a secondary person with a reserved, even dull, approach to their work will inspire the interest of transferring pupils and their parents will be slim while a primary liaison teacher with the same qualities will find it difficult to convey the sense of positive excitement and challenge that the transition process should engender. The enthusiasm of the liaison teachers (so long as it isn't overdone to the extent that their colleagues begin to avoid them!) will also be vital to secure the cooperation of teachers in their own and in their partner schools.

Finally it will also be important for the liaison person to have a reason-able flair for organization. Joint activities involving, say, visits of primary school children to a secondary school, can flop drastically when key people are not properly briefed and prepared, when facilities are not ready, closed or understaffed or when times and dates present difficulties for the hosts or visitors. A smoothly organized event makes its own positive impression in addition to the interpersonal and awareness-raising gains that are made.

Summary

The main steps in developing a liaison programme are summarized below, along with specific suggestions or examples where appropriate.

1   Agree school-based objectives for the proposed liaison programme, e.g.:

   • to inform and advise parents and pupils of transfer options (primary);
   • to portray the school in a manner attractive to prospective pupils and their parents (secondary);
   • to ensure a smooth transition for leaving/incoming pupils.

2   Identify a liaison teacher who is:

   • a good communicator;
   • diplomatic;
   • enthusiastic;
   • organizationally competent.

3   Decide what provision needs to be made for the acclimatization of 'transition' pupils (primary and secondary) and the induction of new pupils (secondary). Consider:

- visits from Year 6 pupils to secondary school sports days, drama productions, fêtes etc.;
- visits from Year 6 pupils during school days (secondary);
- occasional joint teaching arrangements;
- joint Year 6/secondary pupil projects or other learning activities;
- visits by liaison teacher (secondary) to primary schools;
- appointing formal induction support teachers (secondary).

4   Decide what provision needs to be made for the supply of information to parents. Consider:

- a good quality and interesting brochure containing reports of pupil achievements, photographs of staff and pupils, details of school history etc. (secondary);
- collective and individual meetings with parents to inform them about and discuss transfer arrangements, choices of schools (primary meetings) and own school (secondary meetings).

5   Decide what provision needs to be made for professional liaison with colleagues in partner schools. Consider:

- agreement on what information should be transferred and how this transfer should be accomplished (e.g. through ICT etc.);
- meetings between Year 6 and Year 7 teachers (and heads of department) of English, mathematics and science to establish common understanding of curriculum continuity, progression and levels of performance, and the precise curriculum content on both sides of transition (experiments carried out, books read etc.).

6   Put decisions from steps 3–5 into operation simultaneously!

Chapter 7

What is happening in your school?

Issues
- Conducting an audit of existing transition arrangements
- Identifying the key personnel in the transition context
- Identifying areas for change and/or improvement

This chapter considers how schools can assess their existing transition arrangements with a view to consolidating and improving their practice. An audit approach is proposed and the various issues involved in carrying out such an in-house study are discussed. In essence it is important to assess the status quo in relation to transition arrangements and then to build from there. This requires careful planning of the audit itself, including the objectives it is designed to achieve. There is also need for a thorough fact-finding and consultation process with colleagues, other schools, parents and pupils. The chapter sets out the steps necessary to conduct and gain insights from a successful audit.

Introduction

What is your school doing to manage the transition from Year 6 to Year 7? Some secondary schools are highly organized and, for example, place pupils from the same primary schools in the same classes, use 'buddy' systems (in which older pupils look after the new 'recruits') and put on induction days for intending pupils before they start. Some primary schools add to the statutory transfer of information by arranging visits to the secondary schools for their pupils and parents, and/or by inviting the local secondary schools to send representatives or to present mini exhibitions at their school to 'show themselves off'. Very often such arrangements grow into joint events (plays, concerts etc.) or curricular partnerships in which, for example, the secondary school provides access for the primary pupils to their computing facilities or the secondary pupils write newsletters about their school for the primary pupils and so on.

As time goes on it becomes increasingly clear that the days of simply seeing the children out of the door at the end of primary schooling and waiting for a new cohort to arrive in first form are very much over. The theme of partnership in providing the best education for each child pervades all of education and the transition from primary to secondary is a clear example of its importance. This chapter aims to cover the main issues that primary and secondary school partnerships need to consider when assessing their own transition and induction arrangements through in-house audits. The context and content of an audit related to Year 6 and 7 issues are examined in detail and various areas for investigation and questions to be asked are suggested. The chapter includes examples of how an audit may be conducted and how the ensuing information may be used to construct action plans.

As might be expected there is a range of issues relevant to a variety of schools that has to be considered. From the outset, it is important to state that not all areas need to be considered in one go, nor do answers to all of the questions need to be found in order to audit transition procedures. Each section of this chapter should be seen as a guide to 'What is (or is not) happening in my school?'.

Planning for an audit

Planning smooth and successful transition arrangements requires careful analysis and a structured approach. If it is to succeed, you need to start from where the transition programme currently is and you must establish where the developments and changes are needed before any initiative is implemented. As argued above, an audit is the starting point in this process.

An audit of transition and induction arrangements will involve investigating and perhaps questioning existing practice in a coherent and systematic way. Comparing what the transition programme is striving to achieve with what is actually happening between Year 6 and 7 will help clarify the strengths and weaknesses in the system, and will help guide the actions necessary to make the arrangements more effective. A transition audit can therefore be considered to have at least three goals: establishing and clarifying existing transition procedures, identifying strengths to be consolidated and weaknesses to be rectified, and providing a basis for deciding on development priorities. The first of these, the status quo, requires a systematic examination of the school context.

The audit context

For an audit to be successful it is essential to plan it carefully and this planning will be most effective if it clearly takes into account the context in which it is being conducted. It almost goes without saying, therefore, that a transition audit should be set squarely within the school's own ethos;

determined by its mission statement and values and in sympathy with the mission and values of its partner (primary or secondary) schools. Proposals for transition arrangements which do not accommodate such fundamental issues will probably flounder very quickly while proposals which are couched in terms of established school policies will be more familiar to colleagues and parents alike – and more likely to succeed because of that.

Other aspects of the context of the school will include the pupils' and parents' perspectives. Where do most of the children leaving the primary school choose to go or where do most of the first form intake to the secondary school come from? What expectations are there in the local community? New arrangements must obviously build on such patterns and any proposed changes to transition arrangements which might conflict with custom and practice should be carefully weighed up.

The context external to the partnerships must also be carefully assessed. There are statutory obligations on primary schools in relation to the transfer of information on pupils and your school will be complying with these in some manner. Many local authorities will also have implemented transition procedures with which their primary and secondary schools must comply, and if your school is under such an authority your audit must take account of these. In some areas, schools may also have the benefit of recent reviews of transfer procedures, perhaps conducted externally by the local authority or internally by clusters of secondary schools and their feeder primaries.

You will need to gather as much information as you can about the local schools, whether you are a primary school feeding to more than one secondary school or a secondary school receiving from more than one primary school. If partnerships and communications are generally weak between the schools in your area, information on various schools' policies may not be to hand in your school and you may have to carry out some preliminary inquiries to find out what you need. One source of information is the published material about the schools in the locality. For example, local authorities and various trusts might have information about schools registered with them. Schools themselves will often have promotional pamphlets setting out their mission statements, intake criteria etc., and more recently some will have begun to use electronic media (such as web-sites on the World Wide Web) to provide information on the activities in which they engage. There should also be public OFSTED inspection reports of most of the local schools and these can provide valuable information of a different nature, including comment on, in the case of secondary schools, arrangements for inducting new pupils. The much-maligned league tables are also another, albeit limited, source of information.

In summary the preliminary context analysis will require the following pieces of information to be found:

- Are there any aspects of your school's mission or policy that relate, or could relate, to leaving or incoming pupils?
- If you are in a primary school, how are the statutory transfer requirements being met?
- If you come under a local education authority, are there any LEA requirements relating to transfer between schools and if so, how are they met?
- To which schools do your pupils go or from which schools do your pupils come?

Once you have your background work done you must next consider what aspects you will need your audit to cover.

The audit content

The content of your audit should comprise all of the key issues involved in transition management. Such issues as induction procedures, record keeping, school visits etc. may require their own discrete audits to be carried out by different people, or the audit may deal with them all in one process. Whatever the mechanism the ultimate goal is a clear analysis of existing arrangements and necessary future developments. Whether you are in a primary school or a secondary school, there are identifiable areas that should be considered within the transition programme and these may be summarized in a series of questions:

- What transfer procedures exist?
- Are any induction procedures in operation?
- Are there any professional links between associated schools?
- Are there curriculum-related consultations across the transition boundary?
- Is there any overlap in teaching styles and methods?
- What systems are used to deal with pupil records?
- What records are used at transfer and what use is made of them?
- How is progression and continuity mapped?
- How are parents included in the transfer processes?

Many of these questions necessarily involve a degree of overlap as they incorporate strategic issues within any transition programme. Any overlap, however, is likely to be beneficial as it will mean that important aspects should receive regular review. A rolling programme of review and audit is a prerequisite to ensuring you know what is going on in your school and in the schools associated with you. These questions are considered in turn below.

What transfer procedures exist?

In many areas of the country, primary and secondary schools have striven to establish strong partnerships between each other. The motivation for many of these developments has been a combination of educational concern – that pupils have sufficient support and guidance in moving to and establishing themselves in a new school – and self-interest – ensuring that the levels of enrolment are kept up. Other areas and individual schools may not have any such links or may only be beginning to form them.

Whether there are strong links or not, it is important that your audit should establish the nature of any processes, however limited, that do exist and how they may be developed to provide a more effective practice. Well coordinated links would be expected to have the following features:

- identified members of staff in the primary and secondary schools have responsibility for transfer arrangements with a communication process between them well established;
- the primary and secondary headteachers meet regularly to discuss and review transfer procedures which are then disseminated to those involved in implementing them;
- teachers from the primary and secondary schools regularly visit each other's schools;
- the primary teachers have opportunities to visit the secondary schools after transfer to assist in the induction and evaluation of progress of the Year 7 pupils;
- the primary teachers are consulted on how the pupils may be allocated to teaching groups in Year 7;
- documentation over and above the statutory transfer information, and agreed by the secondary schools as being helpful to them, is available from the primary schools.

These areas focus on essential elements that will help to make transfer procedures more effective. It therefore makes sense to include consideration of them when designing an audit of your own school's transition arrangements. If they don't already exist they may be the subject of recommendations arising from the audit.

Are any induction procedures in operation?

Effective induction arrangements are fundamental aspects of successful transition processes and whether you are in a primary or secondary school your audit must attempt a clear description of any systems that are in place. Induction can take many forms and schools are increasingly innovative in their approach. There are, however, some key aspects that an audit should seek to assess. For example, if you are in a primary school, do your Year 6 pupils have the opportunity of visiting their chosen new schools prior to leaving? Do the secondary schools to which your pupils go have induction days? Do your pupils have an opportunity to discuss their experiences, hopes and fears on their return?

If you are in a secondary school, do you run induction days? If so, what activities are covered? For example do you organize meetings with the Year 7 form teacher or visits to the Year 7 form room (if there is one)? Do you organize sample lessons for your visitors or do you arrange for them to meet with present Year 7 pupils? Are the parents of your new intake involved in the induction process and if so what format does their involvement take?

Are there any professional links between associated schools?

Modern educational thinking would argue that developing professional links must contribute to supporting continuity in pupils' learning and their long-term progress. The existence of strong partnerships between schools is highly desirable and the extent of any links, or lack of them, needs to be considered by both the primary and secondary schools in a systematic way. Both sides of the transition have to be involved if effective links are to be developed and sustained. SCAA suggest that:

> The introduction of the National Curriculum has meant discussions on continuity in pupils' learning between associated schools are no longer dominated by the need to establish agreement about the content of the primary school curriculum. The focus for this dialogue can now shift to professional considerations of such matters as the expectations of pupils' performance at the point of transfer and the organisation and sequencing of materials to be taught in Years 6 and 7.
>
> (1996: 13)

This statement is an indication of the types of activities in which schools should be engaging or at the very least attempting to develop. Discussions about the various pupils' stages of development in the programmes of study are one aspect of such professional liaison, while dovetailing the Year 7 teaching and learning with what has been experienced in Year 6 is perhaps the most important and obvious focus. As a means of enhancing pupil learning through a continuity of experience across the transition, joint activities (for example with teachers from primary schools observing secondary teaching, and vice versa) are particularly effective. Differing teaching styles and strategies can be observed, recognized and used to develop awareness of the settings from which pupils are coming or to which they are going.

SCAA (1996) identify four areas in which Year 6 and Year 7 teachers could usefully engage in joint activity and we have couched them in question format to suit an audit context:

How do current arrangements...

- ...foster a better understanding of the continuous nature of learning from primary through to secondary school?
- ...ensure that pupils' previous experiences and achievements are recognized and valued?
- ...ensure that pupils experience appropriately challenging work which builds on the skills, knowledge and understanding acquired in previous Key Stages?
- ...ensure that similarities and connections with prior learning are made explicit?

These are difficult areas to deal with in a single-sided audit (i.e. in the primary school or in the secondary school alone) and really require significant cross-phase cooperation in order to determine the answers. If even one school, your school, takes on the posing of such questions and successfully finds answers, however disappointing the answers might be, the results can be of considerable value to developing an effective transitions programme or improving what already exists. The process of inquiry itself, carried out in a diplomatic and perhaps even informal manner, will promote collaboration and mutual benefit between teachers in both phases through developing knowledge of each other's practice and working culture. This in the long term can consolidate partnership approaches and should therefore contribute to pupils' continued progress across the transition.

Analysing the nature and quality of any professional links existing between your school and your partner schools, whether these are formally established partnerships or simply schools which your pupils go to or come from, requires detailed inquiries on a number of issues and most notably in terms of the continuity of curriculum experience.

Are there curriculum-related consultations across the transition boundary?

Weston, Barrett and Jamison (1992) suggest that a key obstacle to developing curriculum continuity is the lack of fit between curriculum coverage (what is to be learned) and curriculum process (how it is learned), between the contrasting forms of curriculum organization traditionally to be found in primary and secondary schools. Put simply the subject-based approach of the secondary school is considered to be sufficiently different to the cross-curricular approach of the primary school as to cause problems for continuity across the phases. It is argued, however, that the National Curriculum has provided a framework in which the discontinuity can be addressed. Clearly the effective transfer of pupils at the end of Key Stage 2 demands that the theoretical continuity of learning between phases be made practical and real.

An audit can assist in this area by making explicit the relationship between learning in the primary and secondary school. Clearly this can only be achieved if teachers are aware of what has already been taught and what will be taught when pupils arrive at their new school. For continuity to occur discussions must be held between Year 6 and Year 7 teachers with a view to reducing overlap and repetition. Your audit of subject liaison should therefore try to establish the nature and extent of any consultation. For example, is there any subject-based consultation between your colleagues and colleagues in your partner schools? Are programmes of study planned together for Year 6 and Year 7? Are there any arrangements for teachers from each phase to share practice or to observe each other's approach to lessons?

Is there any overlap in teaching styles and methods?

Differences in teaching style lend themselves to what Tickle (1985) has termed 'planned discontinuity'. On transfer to a secondary school, pupils encounter forms of specialist teaching from, say, scientists, historians or geographers which they may have not experienced previously. The difference in experience between usually having one class teacher virtually all day every day in the primary schools and perhaps as many as ten or more specialist teachers in secondary schools at different times each day, must have an impact on how pupils perceive the learning environment to which they transfer. For many pupils the pace of learning and external exam pressures in secondary schools may mean they experience a more instructional 'didactic' approach with less time for discussion and personal autonomy in their learning. If this is the case it may be important for the primary school side of the transition to establish the types of teaching-style pupils may experience on transfer and to try to 'acclimatize' them to it.

Some aspects of secondary experience will be predictable, for example the laboratory environment for science. An audit in a strong partnership arrangement might simply record that the facility exists to provide pupils with experience of various teaching styles and contexts on pre-transfer induction days or fact-finding visits. However, it is just as possible that even well-founded partnerships may not have considered teaching styles and contexts as issues to be addressed. As mentioned above, jointly organized observations of teaching in each other's schools and classes can inform everyone of the likely differences and overlaps in teaching styles and contexts, enabling acclimatization measures to be taken as appropriate. This may mean the pupils taking part in sample lessons on visits to their prospective schools, or viewing videos of teaching in these schools prior to transfer. Each of these approaches is proving popular and indeed some schools will use both to meet their partnership commitments. Understanding the existing situation and working to increase the readiness of pupils by these and other measures may have the added benefit of contributing to an increase in the range of teaching styles within both phases.

There are many other areas affecting children's learning and experience that would benefit greatly from sound liaison between schools across the transition boundary. For example, discussion – rather than simple written information transfer – about pupils with special needs and how they have been or will be met would be a much enhanced means of supporting such children. More generally, positively disposed discussion of all of the transferring pupils' progress would tend to augment planning of the first stage of induction teaching. This approach could extend, some would argue *should* extend, to potentially more negatively disposed discussion of behavioural problems for some children. Great care, however, must be taken to prevent any special attention for such pupils arising from prejudgements being made by receiving teachers. Such attention, regardless how well intended it might be, might actually encourage the extension of previous behaviour instead of enabling a 'new leaf' to be turned through taking nothing for granted and treating all the pupils alike.

What systems are used to deal with pupil records?

The statement below, taken from the SCAA document on 'Promoting Continuity between Key Stage 2 and Key Stage 3', indicates that schools have a statutory requirement to pass on pupil records.

The transfer report on pupils' achievements must contain as a minimum, the following information:

- the pupil's end of Key Stage 1 task/test results (where available) for English and mathematics;
- the pupil's end of Key Stage 1 teacher assessment levels in English, mathematics and science;
- the pupil's end of Key Stage 2 test/task results in English, mathematics and science;

- the pupil's end of Key Stage 2 teacher assessment levels in English, mathematics and science.

(SCAA 1996: 6)

No precise mechanisms for transferring the information are set down and clearly any systems that do exist need to be regularly evaluated, primarily to ensure they meet the secondary schools' needs but also to ensure that they remain manageable for the primary schools. In order to determine if an effective system is in place, your audit will need to consider the following questions:

- What type of information is required by the secondary schools, e.g. do they wish to have pastoral information in addition to the mandatory information on pupils' progress in specific curriculum areas?
- In what fashion do secondary schools prefer the information to be organized and recorded? Is electronic transmission possible and desirable? Is there an agreed format for all schools in the partnership or locality?
- Is there a set timetable for the transfer of the information and, if so, how is this timetable agreed?
- Are there systems in place for the transfer of confidential material concerning individual pupils?

If you are in a secondary school it will quickly become obvious to you that any records you receive from the primary schools will be maximally useful to you and your colleagues if they communicate the type of information you need and in a format which you and your colleagues can use. Equally if you are in a primary school, you must know what type of information the secondary teachers need and the purposes to which they need to put it.

The unavoidable conclusion is that whether you are in a primary or a secondary school you will need to collaborate with your partner schools if the audit is to be of benefit to both parties. However the interests of the transferring pupils are best served by the secondary schools having sufficient and relevant information from the primary schools. In this sense the transition partnership is dependent on the quality of the information coming from the primary school and the quality of the use to which it is put in the receiving secondary school(s). Secondary schools must therefore establish and clearly convey their information needs to their primary partners, ensuring that what they seek is manageable within the primary schools' resources.

Generally speaking, secondary schools need information on their incoming pupils that enables them to make decisions about how the new intake can be grouped. This would normally include pastoral information, for example about friendships existing in the primary schools. If the secondary school has this information they can exploit the settling effects of entering a new situation with friends by placing them in the same classes. Academic information is clearly vital, perhaps to stream entrants but more usually to inform planning of the curriculum and teaching in the pupils' first year. Often this latter type of information is required before the results from the Key Stage 2 assessments are available. This time-lag has the potential to cause problems but many schools get around them by adopting a two-stage process for exchanging information: the first involving teacher assessments (in spring say) and the second combining the final teacher assessments and the end-of-Key Stage results in the summer term.

If your audit does not identify an effective process for the transfer of information then you should ensure that it provides the basis for putting one into effect. An effective system for transfer of information between primary and secondary schools will probably be based on agreement on a two-stage transfer of information, as suggested above, and on the content for the material to be transferred. For example this might include provisional and final teacher assessments in core subjects, information relating to progress in non-core foundation subjects, special needs requirements and so on.

Information on the following should therefore be established through your audit:

- Are there agreed deadlines for the transfer of information? Are these generally met and, if not, are there any particular reasons for them not being met?
- Are there identified people in your school and your partner schools with responsibility for the transfer of information?
- Is the transfer information being disseminated to the appropriate people?
- Would electronic transfer of the information help make dissemination more convenient and effective?
- Are there systems in place to evaluate the use and effectiveness of the information transferred?

This last, relating to the nature and effectiveness of the use made of transfer records, is one which can tread on sensitive areas and your audit approach must be both sensitive and probing. The issues are examined in more detail next.

What records are used at transfer and what use is made of them?

Whether effective use is made of transfer records is sometimes a controversial and emotive issue. Evidence produced from research (Doyle 1997; DfEE Circular 2/96 Report on pupils' achievements in primary schools in 1995/6) shows that a significant number of pupils are given work at inappropriate levels during their first term and indeed some suffer in this manner throughout their first year in secondary school. Such experiences cannot be defended yet they are not uncommon. Serious educational consequences include the possibility of the pupils reacting to unchallenging and perhaps repetitive work by marking time, getting bored and losing interest in school. If the work is too difficult they can perhaps flounder, with any initial pleasure or enthusiasm giving way to frustration, lack of self-esteem and demotivation.

Discontinuity can undoubtedly lead to at least lack of progression in learning and, in the worst case, regression. Clearly it behoves both parts of the partnership to minimize and if possible eradicate the worst effects that a change in schooling can have. On the one hand, if the secondary school is to develop effective systems for progression and continuity of learning for Year 7 pupils, they have to be able to set the level of work as closely as possible to the needs of the incoming pupils. On the other hand, if this to happen, the primary school has to provide as precise information as possible concerning pupils' progress, achievements and levels of attainment. As OFSTED and SCAA have frequently highlighted, however, the 'transfer of records does not in itself ensure that information reaches the appropriate staff, or that it is used effectively' (SCAA 1996: 10).

In comparison to previous years, the Key Stage 2 tests of 1997 were the first to provide a comprehensive set of information for schools involved in the Key Stage 2/3 transition. The additional information included the actual test scores and separate levels in English for Reading and Writing levels. One aim of this extended information was to help with measures to ensure continuity over the transition but the statutory requirement for transfer of information between schools has remained unchanged. The use and dissemination of the additional information is therefore still voluntary rather than obligatory. The extent to which it is used depends on schools liaising and working together in an agreed framework to maximize the data collected. It also requires teachers to be motivated to use records purposefully and professionally.

SCAA suggest that secondary teachers should use transfer records to:

- ensure work is appropriately challenging to all pupils;
- adjust schemes of work and lesson plans to take account of pupils' previous achievements;

- inform decisions about grouping pupils by attainment when such arrangements are used in Year 7;
- reach agreement within a department on the standard and quality of work expected for groups of pupils within different abilities entering the school;
- make specific arrangements for individual pupils (e.g. able pupils, pupils learning English as an additional language or those with special educational needs);
- review the purpose and value of any additional assessment or testing of pupils in Year 7.

(1996: 10)

If you are in a primary school, you will have to find out how any information your school transfers to your partner schools is used; if you are in a secondary school, you will have to find out how the incoming information is disseminated and used by your Year 7 colleagues. A checklist for assessing aspects of the information transfer and receipt would include finding information on:

- the nature and content of the transfer records;
- the manner in which the information is stored;
- the manner in which the records are transferred;
- where responsibility lies for transferring or receiving and disseminating the transfer records;
- the monitoring of the use and effectiveness of the transfer records.

It is also important to remember that the passing on of records is the responsibility of individual schools and it must therefore be in the interest of primary and secondary schools to work together to ensure continuity.

How are progression and continuity mapped?

Theoretically the National Curriculum provides a framework for curriculum continuity but as mentioned above, there is evidence to suggest that this is not yet being fully utilized. Many secondary teachers consider Year 7 as a fresh start rather than a continuation from primary school and clearly this approach does not lend itself well to fostering progression or continuity in learning and attainment. Continuity necessitates the presence of an agreed curriculum plan which bridges the gap between the primary, and lower secondary years of schooling. Continuity also implies agreement at the level of aims and objectives, as well as the selection and organization of content, skills and methods of assessment. Such an agreement requires collaboration and consultation amongst staff responsible for transfer and any audit should set out to assess the extent of these relationships or, in their absence, to propose ways of developing them.

For your audit to inform arrangements for progression and continuity, one way is to carry it out at two levels by considering issues that are school-based and those that are individual pupil-based. Assessment of the various school-based issues will require you to engage in dialogue with colleagues in your partner schools. The areas of interest for your audit will include an assessment of the extent and nature of any overlap, particularly in the core subjects of English, mathematics and science, between Year 6 and Year 7. If there is any commonality between them is it likely to be repetition, consolidation or progression? Are there any formal staff consultations, for example joint staff meetings, to consider schemes of work which underpin continuity and a degree of progression? Are there any opportunities for observation or joint teaching visits between colleagues in your school and your partner schools?

Assessment and reporting of pupil progress is another important aspect on which to seek detailed information. For example, in the individual subject areas, how is progression and continuity monitored in your school and your partner schools? Is there a common understanding of assessment procedures between your school and your partner schools? This can be a very important aspect of liaison. If the nature of the assessment procedures and outcomes is not known, continuity will suffer. Similarly a common understanding of standards between your colleagues and colleagues in your partner schools is vital. For example, is a Level 4 in science in the primary school considered to be Level 4 in the secondary school, and if not do any processes exist to develop shared understanding of the standards involved?

Collecting the evidence on these school-based related issues will help form the basis of action plans for developing and sustaining school policies, particularly in the secondary side of the partnership. It will also foster continuity in teaching and learning and it is vital to consider how these issues relate to individual pupils.

> Continuity is what is or is not experienced by the individual child. He or she is the one who experiences the discontinuity of demands made by different teachers and different schools.
>
> (Dean 1988: 51)

More specific questions, at the level of the individual pupil's experience and which the audit might ask of the receiving secondary schools, would therefore usefully include:

• Is there a means of monitoring a pupil's experience of the early Key Stage 3 curriculum?

- Are any of the teaching and learning methods commonly used in your school unfamiliar to any of the pupils?
- How is the progress of individual pupils assessed, recorded and reported and does this complement the pupils' prior experiences of these processes?
- How are individual pupils' special educational needs recorded and met?

Any audit that takes place must identify the issues related to progression and continuity and ask the types of questions presented above, if the pupils' experience and learning achievements are to be enhanced.

How are parents included in the transfer processes?

Many of the anxieties felt during the transfer process relate to parents as well as to pupils. Parents' attitudes can significantly influence both their children's performance and their expectations and it is therefore essential that they are kept fully informed of transfer procedures at each step in the process. Transfer is a traumatic time for all involved and can be compounded by a variety of procedures that may be local, such as selection (e.g. 11+), or national such as Key Stage 2 Standard Attainment Tasks. Primary and secondary schools must take responsibility for informing parents adequately to enable the choice of school to be an informed rather than an *ad hoc* decision.

In relation to the primary school, a variety of questions needs to be examined and answered by your audit. These include:

- What arrangements are in place to help the parents of your transferring pupils to choose the appropriate secondary school for their children?
- Does your school provide parents with any documentation on the transfer procedures? If so, is the effectiveness of this documentation regularly reviewed?
- Are the headteachers of the local secondary schools, or their representatives, invited to your school to talk to the parents of your transferring pupils?
- If selection occurs at 11 are the parents of your transferring pupils informed of the procedures and implications of selection? If no, how can an information process be introduced and what should it comprise?
- If selection takes place do the parents of your transferring pupils understand the distinction between the selection tests and the standard assessment tasks?

- Are the parents of your transferring pupils informed of any appeal procedures they can pursue if their child does not gain a place in the school of their choice?
- Should an appeal arise, are the parents involved given any assistance?

If you are in a secondary school, your audit will usefully consider the following issues when auditing parental choice and liaison procedures:

- How is the school promoted among the parents of potential Year 7 recruits?
- Does the school have an open day/evening etc. for the parents of prospective pupils, prior to their making a choice of school?
- Does the school send representatives to primary schools on transfer information days/evenings etc.?

Once children have been allocated a place in your school the following should be considered in terms of liaising with parents:

- What information do parents receive in relation to their children taking up a place in the school?
- Is there an opportunity for parents and pupils to visit the school prior to the school year starting? Are any special induction events organized, for example during the summer break, to introduce the new pupils to the school and their future colleagues?
- Is there an induction process (for example, open days or evening receptions) for new parents?
- How are parents made aware of the school's expectations of the pupils in Year 7?
- Are parents aware of the lines of communication between themselves and the school?

Finding appropriate answers to the questions above, or recommending appropriate action if none exist, can help secondary schools formulate policies which will enhance the transfer process from a pastoral and academic perspective. Well informed parents can provide constructive support for their children to help them acclimatize to the transition from Key Stage 2 to Key Stage 3.

Once you are happy that you have a good grasp of the context of your audit, and that you have identified the issues that it must address, you must begin to think about how you will conduct it.

The audit strategy

This section considers how you might go about your audit of your school's and your partner schools' approaches to transition. One immediate concern relates to the audience for the audit. Who do you intend should read and act upon the audit? The approach you decide to take may be influenced to a greater or larger extent by your intended audience. For example if it is for internal consumption by colleagues in your own school, you should have some freedom to assume aspects of the matter are already common currency and therefore need little explanation or direct attention. On the other hand, if it is a wider audience – even an audience quite close to 'home' such as the board of governors of your school – you will need to ensure that you do not make unreasonable assumptions about the level of familiarity they have in relation to the various matters covered by the audit (e.g. relationships with partner schools).

Bearing in mind the issue of audience, the next strategic concern is to consider the methods you will use to meet your audit objectives. There is a wide variety of methods available and the aim should be to choose those that are appropriate, functional and practical for the situation. The two main strategies are (i) to hand the matter over, with a detailed brief, to external 'auditors', or (ii) to carry it out internally. In the latter case you may choose to employ a published audit scheme, such as that suggested in this book, or you may design your own approach to suit better the needs of your own school's context.

Whichever strategy you choose, clearly it must address the questions that need to be answered and be feasible within the time-scale available. In relation to the former it is therefore essential to identify the audit's scope i.e. who will be the sources of information and what information will be sought? The concern about time is particularly relevant if you are conducting the audit alone and in addition to your normal duties and responsibilities. Your chosen strategy should also be acceptable to those who are most likely to be involved, for example colleagues in Year 6 or Year 7, others with responsibility for transfer or induction and those with general responsibility and authority in school affairs – for example the school's management team and the board of governors.

An external audit

External perspectives can be very useful, particularly in bringing an explicitly objective eye to the processes of transfer, or indeed the lack of them. An external auditor can be expected to evaluate the matter from a different angle than those involved in the school and they may also bring insights and operational ideas from their experience of practice in other schools. However, anyone commissioned to carry out an independent audit must be well-briefed in terms of the remit they are required to address and must be familiar with the customs and practice and indeed mission of your school.

Each strategy has its own strengths and weaknesses. The use of an external auditor reduces the demands made on staff and can provide impartial advice to schools. Their terms of reference can also be 'formative' i.e. they can be asked to encourage staff not just to supply information for the audit but also to question the whole process and, in particular, aspects that they may have been taking for granted. Care needs to be taken that the audit stays on track (usually with regular feedback meetings) and that it does probe the issues in sufficient depth i.e. that the auditor(s) do not take things for granted. The content and language of any audit report must be 'palatable' i.e. it should not alienate those people who will probably be charged with taking forward any new or improved activities it recommends.

An internal audit

For most schools, the option of an externally conducted audit will probably be a luxury they cannot afford but an internally conducted audit should never, as a consequence, be thought of as second best. On the contrary, the very features that might be argued as the benefits of an externally conducted audit (e.g. objectivity and experience of other systems of working) can be more than adequately compensated for by the insider knowledge and the commitment to an improved system that an internally conducted audit can provide. If you choose an internal audit you will not be making additional demands on those most involved in it – for example the Year 6 or Year 7 teachers as appropriate – as they will shoulder the same burdens in answering questions for an internal as for an external audit.

Strategies for any kind of audit centre on the primary task of gathering information relating to the audit focus. Normally an audit will consider an organization's procedures, and any externally imposed procedures, and will evaluate how well the organization complies with them. In the case of transition processes there might be very comprehensive arrangements, some minimal procedures or indeed no procedures in existence at all. Compliance therefore is not the main issue. Rather it will be the goal of your audit to identify the extent and nature of any arrangements designed to manage the transition of pupils between Year 6 and Year 7. The audit methods will therefore involve the collection of information from sources inside and outside your own school and will often depend on a balance between accessibility or convenience and the importance of the information to your quest. For example the views of the parents of the pupils who are transferring from your school or who are coming into the school as the new intake will be particularly important. However, if there are say 100 pupils involved you are less likely to consider a chat with each set of parents than perhaps a questionnaire for all of them, backed up by a sample of interviews; if there are only thirty pupils you might consider interviewing all of the parents, and so on.

Similarly, if there are likely to be large numbers of colleagues in your own school and in your partner schools, who are involved in some way with transfer arrangements, you might consider identifying some key people for a chat; choosing a questionnaire to try to capture the views of the others that you cannot get the time to get around. Special forms of questionnaire may be required for each type of teacher: for example heads of mathematics, English and science in the secondary schools, headteachers or Year 6 teachers in the primary schools.

The use of questionnaires allows every member of staff involved in the transition process to be surveyed but unless it can be taken 'off the shelf', the drawing up of the questionnaires can take up a considerable amount of time. Off the shelf material may look more professional and the generality of the questions may also be accepted more readily as an impartial quest for information. However the very generality will frequently mean that the questions asked are not specific enough for the needs of your school or the context in which it finds itself. For example, awkward or irrelevant questions may be asked of parents or the tone may be viewed as impersonal and intrusive by colleagues in your partner schools. Designing your own audit questionnaires and interview schedules should generate a more personal approach and your knowledge of the context should enable you to frame your questions in such a way that they are more easily answered by your respondents.

Your audit may also exploit a number of different ways of talking to people to collect their views. You may, for example, find it useful to hold meetings with your target groups. Such events might include a one-day conference for schools in your area hosted by your own school, training days for your colleagues with invitations to colleagues in partner schools or informal evening meetings with parents. Alternatively, or in addition, you might arrange to observe induction arrangements in your partner secondary schools or, if you are in a secondary school, in other schools in your area. A combination of techniques will usually produce a more accurate and in-depth picture of the status quo than a relatively brief or superficial survey alone.

Meetings

Meetings are an obvious way of gathering information from different schools or departments but if they are to be a central strategy in your audit process it is important that they are well planned. For example, all participants should be provided with information for discussion before-hand. They should be aware of the objectives of the meeting and how their contribution should help to achieve them. The meetings should aim to arrive at some form of conclusion or decision by ensuring that the discussions are well structured and have a clear focus. Participants in your meetings should leave feeling that they have been able to contribute their views and ideas and you must ensure that the actual discussions are inclusive and not simply 'hogged' by a vociferous few. Finally you should arrange to draw up a summary of the discussion for circulation to all involved, especially if you wish to continue the exercise in more depth later.

Interviews

Interviews are generally the most useful means of collecting information on an individual level. They can be conducted in a number of ways and the chosen mode will depend on the nature of the information you wish to collect and the context and constraints under which the interview is to be completed. If you are planning an interview approach in your audit you must first consider what information you need and who is likely to provide it. Crucially you must set down the questions you feel will lead to the answers you need to collect. Once you know what it is you want to find out, who it is that you will get the information from and what questions you need to ask, you can then decide on the best mode of interview. Again expedience may be a big factor. Time and convenience issues will affect your respondents as much as yourself and you will need to decide whether parents, for example, can meet you one-to-one or perhaps as a group for an informal discussion. Access to colleagues in other schools, and also perhaps in your own school, may require permission from the headteacher of the school concerned – the prospect of someone from another school investigating operational arrangements in any area of school policy is unlikely simply to be ignored by that school's managers! And even if you think you will probably not need official approval you would be well advised to check it out, as a matter of courtesy if nothing else.

In terms of good practice, one-to-one and group interview sessions have a number of features in common. Firstly, if you have not had an opportunity to brief the people concerned in writing, and even if you have, you should always begin by explaining the purpose of the interview or discussion. This initial stage should be aimed at relaxing your respondent(s) – an informal context with soft seating, coffee or tea will greatly assist in creating the right ambience. You may be tempted to record the dialogue but in most cases, if you have structured your own thinking and approach properly, you should get sufficient information by listening and taking brief notes. If you are managing an audit rather than conducting it entirely by yourself, then you should ensure that anyone carrying out interviews on your behalf holds to these same principles.

Group interviews (often called *focus group* interviews) can be more difficult to manage and analyse than one-to-one interviews. Managing them requires you to ensure that the group does not go off at tangents to the main discussion themes and that everyone gets a chance to contribute. You may have to call upon reserves of diplomacy to moderate the contribution of the most participative members of the group and to open up those who are most reticent! The analysis can be quite complex as you seek to identify the issues on which the group agrees (convergence), those for which there is a clear difference of opinion (divergence), or those for which no particular opinion is expressed at all.

Questionnaires

Questionnaires are often used to collect information quickly from large or widely disparate groups of people. Although questionnaires seem to be straightforward they often take a long time to construct. Good questionnaires are very effective but all too often if questionnaires are badly constructed they can lead to a poor quality of information being collected. The first step in questionnaire design is always to decide to whom it is being addressed and what information needs to be obtained from it. Are there enough people involved to warrant the design of a questionnaire or would a series of brief, after-school meetings cover everyone whose views you need to gather?

If you decide on a questionnaire approach will it be one questionnaire or a series of questionnaires tailored for different people? For example, it would seem obvious that the questions in relation to transfer that you might wish to ask a school principal will be somewhat different than those you would ask a receiving Year 7 teacher or a Year 6 teacher whose pupils are moving on. It is possible to design one overall questionnaire but so much of it will appear redundant to any one type of respondent that it may be dismissed without being completed.

Questionnaire design is exhaustively covered in the research literature and you may wish to refer to some such sources. The design guidelines that follow will, however, provide sufficient information for a 'common-sense' approach.

The questions asked in a questionnaire need to be quite specific – primarily because you will not be there to enlarge on them but also because you want to get unambiguous answers. There are essentially two question types: closed and open. A closed question will offer a number of set answers from which the respondent can choose e.g. for a primary school audit:

Does your school organize (*tick as many responses as appropriate*):

- curriculum progression meetings between your colleagues and Year 7 colleagues in your partner secondary schools? ☐
- reciprocal teaching visits between your colleagues and colleagues in your partner schools? ☐
- visits to your partner schools by prospective Year 7 pupils? ☐
- transfer information events for parents? ☐
- ...etc.

An open question, sometimes called a free response question, will demand that the respondents think for a bit and then construct an answer in their own words. This latter type of question is particularly powerful if you want to get at people's views but haven't the time or access to sit and discuss with them. An example for a secondary school audit might be:

- What information do you as head of department wish to receive in relation to Year 7 pupils?

Questionnaire design will normally require a pilot phase in which you test the structure and the questions themselves with a group of people, representative of those to whom you will administer the completed instrument. The pilot testing should ensure that the content, wording and sequencing of the questions, and any fixed choice responses, will be understood unambiguously by the target respondents. The piloting will also ensure that what you are asking people to do is reasonable and does not require undue amounts of time either to answer the questions directly or to seek information in order to answer them.

Observation

As has been argued above, and recommended by bodies such as SCAA, wherever possible primary and secondary teachers working within the transition interface should observe the teaching in each other's schools. Understanding differences in culture, context, teaching styles and strategies can be very important for all concerned with Year 6 and 7 pupils. In a similar fashion, if you want to add depth to your audit, you might choose to use observation as a method of gathering information on how other schools handle transfer and induction arrangements. This might include observing how information meetings for parents, open days for parents and prospective pupils, induction days for first formers only etc. are handled by schools in your area. Again it is imperative that you follow the conventional courtesy of requesting the permission of the managers of the school(s) you are intending to visit. You must also have a clear idea why you are carrying out an observation visit. It might be that you wish to see how arrangements you know exist are actually put into effect or it might be that you are simply looking for ideas to bring back into your own school. It is time-consuming to act as an observer at complex social events so you will wish to maximize the benefits you get from the visits by drawing up a brief list of issues and processes on which you want to collect ideas or information.

Choosing your own approach to an audit allows you to focus on issues that are of particular importance to your school and your partner schools. If you are managing an audit (i.e. other colleagues are conducting parts of it using a team approach), you will have to ensure that all angles are covered by careful planning of the audit itself and by choosing the people and their roles carefully.

The auditors

If you are intending to conduct an internal audit i.e. one that is not going to be commissioned from external agencies, you may be planning to carry it out alone or you may be intending to adopt a team approach. Whichever is the case it does well to consider a number of design matters before making a firm decision. Several questions should be addressed:

- Which aspects of the transition process are to be audited and can I accomplish the whole process alone? If not, who is best placed to carry each aspect forward?
- If others are to be involved in a team approach what will their roles be and how will they be briefed?
- If others are to be involved will you or someone else be charged with drawing the various parts together? How will this be best served?

Each aspect of an audit requires a lead person with a clear view of what is expected and of the time-scale necessary to achieve it. If that person is always the same person (you!), then the need for briefing and role clarification is obviated. Let us assume for a moment, however, that a team approach is both desirable and achievable. The likely members of such a team in a secondary school will be different from a primary school team. In the secondary school there may be a relatively large team comprising, for example, the head of junior school or equivalent, the head of Year 7 and the Year 7 teachers of the core subjects: mathematics, English and science. In contrast the team in the primary school could well comprise the principal and one other.

It is the Year 6 teacher (or, in large primary schools, the head of Year 6) and the head of Year 7 (secondary) who will probably have most to contribute. They are best placed to marshal the information gathering and discussion on issues related to the preparation for transfer on the one hand and the arrangements for recruitment and subsequent induction on the other. They are also best placed to contribute to discussions related to the continuity of the curriculum between the two phases, with particular emphasis on the core areas of mathematics, English and science. Although the lead may come from the secondary school side, both types of people will have an interest in promoting the sharing of experience and scrutiny of the levels of attainment, schemes of work and areas of joint teaching. The cooperation of both the Year 6 and the Year 7 teachers is essential to establish clearly the links between the theory of the curriculum progression framework and the reality of the continuity in learning experience.

Other important members of any team will include representatives of the policy-making levels of the schools – perhaps the principal or a vice-principal but at least members of the senior management of the school who have responsibility for transfer and induction matters and for curriculum development and monitoring. The team leader will be responsible for the important role of collating the various members' contributions and forming them into a succinct and accessible audit report. Put fairly simply the report must address several audiences (staff in the partner schools and perhaps boards of governors, local authority officers, parents etc.) and should minimally cover the following:

- list of partner schools and usual numbers of pupils going to/coming from each year;
- arrangements for receiving and disseminating/sending* transfer information;
- types of information received/sent*;
- arrangements for transfer/induction* information events and activities;
- arrangements for liaison on reciprocal visits and teaching, curriculum progression and so on.

(* dependent on whether primary or secondary)

Presenting the information in an accessible way is an absolute priority to give the audit the best chance of being assimilated by those who will be expected to act upon it. Simply setting down the factual information above, however, will only be half the story – you must also provide a level of analysis and judgement to guide the readers in following it up. Your report should therefore set out simply and succinctly the various features of the transfer arrangements to which your school is party. These will include your judgement of the existing strengths and weaknesses and any gaps or overlaps in the arrangements. You must of course be candid about any limitations in your audit which may have to be picked up at a later date, perhaps under another audit process. The central message of your report should be a view on what areas of activity appear to be effective and what areas may require further developments or improvements. If it is possible to prioritize the development/improvements needs then this will assist the planning process.

A report that is brief yet comprehensive, easy-to-read yet focused, will find much favour in the intended audiences. It should be jargon-free and fair, distinguishing clearly between fact and judgement or opinion, and it should provide clear leads including alternative options for the next phase of activity: the development of an action plan.

An action plan can be considered to have at least four main themes: details of what needs to be done, who will have responsibility for doing it, what resources will be needed for them to do it and when will it be carried out. A good action plan will probably establish priorities and objectives and will set targets for meeting them. It will also offer guidance on how to judge its progress by setting down success criteria against which the various developments and activities can be assessed. A typical action plan might appear as in Table 7.1.

Table 7.1 Action plan on parental liaison

Priority	To improve the school's transition procedures with respect to parental liaison
Target 1	Survey views of the parents, of previous and present years' leavers or intake,* on the nature and quality of liaison
Assessment	(1) Monitor number of parents responding (2) Analyse parents' views from the responses
Target 2	Write policy for parental liaison and inform parents about it through a newsletter
Assessment	(1) Seek parents' views with tear-off evaluation slips in newsletter (2) Seek outside external view on effectiveness of newsletter (3) Seek views of staff and governors
Target 3	Invite parents to open evening related to transition procedures
Assessment	(1) Monitor number of parents attending (2) Seek parents' verbal and written comments on the night
Time	First two terms of year to canvass views and prepare report

(*Table 7.1* cont.)

Dates	(1) Survey parents' views by middle of first term (2) Agree policy internally by end of first term (3) Publish and disseminate newsletter with policy at start of second term (4) Arrange information evening in middle of second term (5) Collate parents' views of policy with information from tear-off slips and verbal feedback at information evening, and views of other groups (staff etc.) by end of second term (6) Prepare amendments arising from collated views and revise policy for internal agreement
Resources	Establish source of funds for newsletter Identify staff, venue and hospitality needs for parents' evening
Coordinator	Identify coordinator for event, policy development etc. (e.g. head of Year 6 or Year 7 or head of lower school)

Notes: * depends on whether primary or secondary

Summary

This chapter has focused on the question 'What is happening in your school?'. It has also discussed ways in which you might look for the answers. Suggestions have been made as to the areas and issues that may need auditing and the questions the audit may need to address. Possible strategies have been highlighted, techniques and methods for collecting information and analysing the information gathered have been suggested. The emphasis throughout has been on the need to draw conclusions and make recommendations through the audit report, with the ultimate aim being to facilitate future action planning and development. Below are some of the key steps in assisting the process:

1 Agree school-based objectives for the proposed audit.
2 Agree any cross-phase objectives (i.e. with partner schools) for the audit.
3 Identify the key personnel who will conduct the audit process.
4 Identify areas for change or improvement and draw up an action plan.

Chapter 8

Collaborative networks for continuity

Issues
- Setting up and managing a collaborative network
- Team approaches to transition arrangements
- Establishing a calendar of events

This chapter draws together the main themes underpinning a collaborative network: the need for continuity and progression across the transition, the timely and relevant transfer of information on pupils' progress and achievements, and the liaison necessary to ensure the transition from Key Stage 2 to 3 is as smooth as possible. The role of management in setting up and providing continuing leadership for the collaboration is set out, and the use of working groups or teams is discussed. Finally a calendar of actions and events for the typical network is proposed.

Introduction

In this final chapter we look at ways schools and teachers can construct a collaborative network to facilitate the transfer of pupils across the Key Stage 2/3 interface. The first step in developing such a collaboration is for the potential partners to meet and agree a common purpose. They must then set about establishing the means to achieving it. Invariably the process will involve negotiation between partners, some of whom may be coming together for the first time. In this latter instance, the initial phase will therefore present opportunities for exploring each other's views and seeking to establish shared meanings and procedures in relation to the transition. While a collaborative approach to transition might begin, and indeed flourish, at the level of one or two teachers in neighbouring schools, we would argue that the long-term future of a collaboration will require management backing and leadership, and it is this issue that we examine first.

Managing a collaborative network

Primary and secondary headteachers and senior staff must give leadership in establishing collaborative structures. This leadership is needed to facilitate and encourage their colleagues to work together in a constructive and purposeful way. The recognition that both phases have a great deal to learn from each other can only be generated if the headteachers from both phases underpin this view and work together in the pursuit of effective transfer practice. Secondary and primary teachers are experts in their own contexts and it is through good management of the collaboration that this expertise can flourish and be brought to bear on curriculum development and transfer arrangements. Continuing success in any collaborative venture will depend on the building of such positive relationships, which in turn will generate further success. They will also offer an effective means to resolve any issues and problems that arise in the course of the transition process.

From a management point of view, the first priority must be to establish contact with colleagues in partner schools. With each secondary school acting as the apex of a pyramid of feeder primary schools it might seem likely that the first move in setting up a collaborative network might come from them. However, this is not always the case. It is common to find clusters of primary schools already sharing peripatetic teachers or other resources and such clusters may then provide a focus for a collaborative approach to transfer arrangements; in this case dealing corporately with a number of secondary schools.

Regardless of who might initiate the development, it is clear that there must be agreement from both perspectives: primary and secondary. Ensuring continuity in pupils' curriculum experience, and progression in both the challenge they are presented with and the levels of performance they achieve, will be the main targets for any collaboration. Underpinning these objectives will be comprehensive measures to ensure the pupils' (and their parents') orientation and induction into the new phase of education on which they are embarking. In order to achieve understanding and agreement on the various issues involved there will therefore need to be a series of meetings between the potential partners. Clearly, it is important that everyone is involved to ensure they 'own' the objectives and the means of achieving them. Any resulting collaboration will therefore be at a level of involvement and sophistication that suits the partners concerned.

Whatever the model of partnership or level of involvement, headteachers will find that a team approach will be needed for each aspect of the transfer programme. Each school will need to identify the people who will take the collaboration forward. In the primary school, the central people will be the Year 6 teacher(s), the headteacher or vice-principal, and a liaison teacher (if different from those already identified). In the secondary school it is likely that there will be a larger pool of people involved. These would normally include the Year 7 teachers along with, perhaps, the heads of the core subjects (and perhaps heads of other subjects), the head of lower school, the teacher in charge of induction, the liaison teacher, the head teacher and so on. Clearly some of these roles may be vested in the same person. Once identified a number of teams must come together to take the work forward. An effective collaborative network will tend, therefore, to have the following teams:

Management team   This will probably comprise the headteachers of the partner schools and its first task will be to review any transfer arrangements that already exist between the partners. They will attempt to identify inadequacies and areas for improvement and will formulate and oversee the implementation of agreed policy within the cooperative structure. The group may also act as an interface between the collaboration and the local authority or other relevant organizations. Once a working collaboration has been initiated, this group will also play an important review and evaluation role to ensure that the system continually develops and renews itself in the light of any changing circumstances.

Operational liaison team   This group will comprise the partner schools' designated liaison teachers and will oversee the all aspects of the collaboration on behalf of their respective schools. They will variously have responsibility for:

- planning the annual programme, including events for transfer pupils and their parents;
- organizing the provision of any necessary resources: financial, personnel, locations etc.;
- joint staff development programmes between the collaboration's partner schools;
- the transfer of timely and relevant information between schools and to transfer pupils and their parents;
- facilitating arrangements to enable teachers to meet and take part in joint teaching visits and other visits involving pupils.

Curriculum liaison teams   There may be three or more of these (e.g. English, mathematics and science) but it must be recognized that the logistics, from the primary school perspective, may rapidly become unmanageable as the same Year 6 teacher(s) have to liaise on all three core areas of the Key Stage 2 curriculum. Where there is only one Year 6 teacher, he or she will probably also be the liaison teacher and the problem of enabling them to join in the various teams will clearly present itself. The secondary school, on the other hand, can be more manageably represented by a selection from the Year 7 teachers and heads of department of the core subjects, with the head of the lower school as an additional alternative.

The key issues teachers must address at these meetings are the demands of the National Curriculum at Key Stage 2 and Key Stage 3. If continuity and progression in learning are to be facilitated, primary teachers need to be aware of the early demands of Key Stage 3, and secondary teachers must have a working knowledge of Key Stage 2. Even with the detailed programmes of study for each subject there is considerable room for flexibility and interpretation and it is therefore vital that no assumptions are made about work in either phase.

Establishing working teams

If any working group begins to feel that their efforts are not considered a priority or are considered relatively unimportant, their effectiveness will be greatly reduced and indeed the collaboration may fall apart. Collaborative teams must therefore have management backing to succeed. The members have to be selected carefully and the work programme needs to be structured to ensure it is manageable in the timeframe set aside for it. Team-building itself takes time and several stages in development can usually be identified, starting at the point at which they are brought together. Tuckman (1985), for example, suggests four phases, which he describes as: 'forming', 'storming', 'norming' and 'performing' respectively.

'Forming'

In this stage the team has just been brought together. Their individual roles in the group may be uncertain and the role of the working group itself may yet be vague, perhaps described in relatively general terms e.g. 'the Liaison Group will bring forward proposals for transfer arrangements'. Some members, perhaps all in some instances, may be anxious about whether they have the experience or the authority to act on behalf of their schools. At this 'forming' stage a relatively close watching brief should be kept by the headteachers/school management team to ensure that the group moves in the desired direction and that each school's interests are properly represented.

'Storming'

The next stage in team-building is the important one of sifting through the variety of possible tasks, problems and objectives that the group might have. A 'brainstorming' approach is often effective with ideas and opinions, on ways forward, being introduced and thoroughly debated in the group. There is the potential for some conflict during this phase and care will need to be taken that the working contexts of primary and secondary schools are properly recognized and respected. A likely area in which differences of opinion may well arise will be the subject- versus child-centred approaches to teaching that the two sectors are often perceived to follow. Aspects of the team's working brief may well require clarification and ideas may be 'bounced off' colleagues, including headteachers, back at each member's school. The ultimate aim must be to ensure that there is collective agreement on the objectives of the group and how they will be achieved. This clarification will be best served by regular feedback from the various representatives to their own colleagues.

'Norming'

The so-called 'norming' stage gets underway once the issues are agreed and the broad means to achieving the group's goals are shared. Everyone in the group adopts the group 'norm' and planning proceeds quickly in a spirit of mutual support and common purpose. The plans and proposals are taken back to each member's school, and if the feedback reporting has been effective, they are quickly agreed and set in motion.

'Performing'

The final 'performing' stage sees a high level of interdependence and trust translated into an effective action programme. Solutions to problems quickly emerge, resources are shared openly and the cooperation generates success as judged from parent, pupil and teacher feedback. This in turn maintains the team spirit and the commitment to collective action.

If starting from scratch, i.e. with no existing arrangements or only rudimentary cooperation on transfer, these stages and meetings may well take quite some time. It must be stressed, however, that a solid foundation is essential for a collaborative network to last; time taken in the early stages, to establish clear understandings and roles, will reap dividends in later working relationships. Once the meetings have been set in motion, and with the basic issues agreed, it may be possible to conduct the bulk of subsequent business at a person-to-person level, keeping the collective meetings to a more manageable schedule, some on a termly, others on an annual basis.

One fundamental ingredient of good working relationships is worth repeating: there must be mutual respect between partners for the collaboration within these teams to succeed. Those directly involved and experienced in liaison will usually have a practical grasp of this simple tenet but others who will have to become involved may need to review how they see colleagues in partner institutions. In many schools little has changed since Derricott felt moved to observe, in relation to the primary/secondary transfer of information, that 'Teachers suspect their colleagues' judgements and prefer to rely on their own diagnosis' (Derricott 1985: 86). As we mentioned in an earlier chapter, one of the most powerful means of ensuring this mutual respect is to engage teachers from each side of the Key Stage 2/3 divide in visiting partner schools and working in their colleagues' classrooms. This is a time-consuming and perhaps expensive measure (e.g. in substituting the visiting teacher's class teaching) but it will provide the basis for building a significant bond between collaborating schools and teachers.

Meetings to initiate collaboration

This team approach to a collaborative network arises from our view that little can be achieved in terms of continuity and progression, and in information transfer and liaison, unless there is a shared awareness of their importance and agreed procedures for achieving them between the partner schools. Whether the initiative comes from a secondary school seeking to promote itself among prospective transfer pupils, or a primary school seeking to improve the transition process for its leaving pupils, there will need to be a series of exploratory meetings to seek the interest and cooperation of the various schools involved. These early meetings should be relatively informal but purposeful, with fixed and previously circulated agendas; taking turns to host the meetings at the various partner school locations will help the early cementing together of the cluster of cooperating schools. It is a good idea to have a fairly wide-ranging discussion of issues in these initial meetings with the more formal meetings following relatively soon afterwards ('forming', 'storming' etc.).

Underpinning collaborative arrangements

The themes of this book: *continuity and progression*, *transfer of information* and *liaison* represent the working context of the framework that will underpin collaboration between partner schools. Agreement on the principles and actions necessary in these areas is vital for contributing to smooth transitions for transfer pupils and much of the business of the teams and meetings noted above will be directed at ensuring it is reached. We shall examine them briefly in turn.

Continuity and progression

In order to establish a successful collaborative framework around transfer arrangements, it is necessary to accept that continuity and progression in learning, and smoothness in transition from one learning environment to another, are the intended outcomes. Continuity, as we have stressed throughout, is vital on a number of counts. It enables teachers, regardless of the year group they are teaching, to build logically on the grasp of various concepts that children bring from all of their previous years of learning. From the children's perspective, it offers them the opportunity to use and develop further the learning and skills they possess. In essence, the pursuit of this logical progression is aimed at limiting repetition and gaps in the pupils' learning. A smooth transition to the next stage is important if success in learning is to be built upon and if weaknesses are to be properly addressed.

Frameworks for collaborative action in the Key Stage 2/3 transition are supported by the design of the National Curriculum. This has given schools an academic 'map' on which to devise strategies for continuity and progression. The basic structure requires teachers, whether they are engaged in the years of Key Stage 1 or are concerned with the transition from Key Stage 3 to 4, to come together on a regular basis and plan the curriculum that they will deliver. Most teachers will point to the increased liaison between teachers, particularly in same-school transitions such as Key Stages 1 to 2 and Key Stage 3 to 4, as a major beneficial outcome of the National Curriculum development. As we have argued throughout, however, Key Stage 2 to 3 liaison (when this means a change of schools) is particularly difficult to organize but is even more important to get right. All Year 6 and 7 teachers need to appreciate – many already do – the value of talking to each other about pupils' achievements, both inside and outside the classroom, in order to limit the negative impacts of this transition as much as possible. When attempting to set up effective procedures to establish continuity, both primary and secondary schools will therefore need to consider each other's values and the ethos within which they plan their curriculum and organize their school day. They will also need to review the teaching strategies they use and the expectations they place on pupils. The very act of being positive about what is going on, and of informing each other, parents and pupils, will probably help to establish open and effective collaborative networks.

Talking alone, however, will not solve the problems of curriculum continuity. What is often missing is that teachers from within and between the phases need to have a good working understanding of the content and delivery of the curriculum either preceding or following their own particular phase of teaching. Teachers on both sides need to accept that, even within a well structured framework of specified objectives, the only guarantee that they will be met is that the objectives themselves should relate to the actual teaching that takes place. Ideally within the framework of collaboration, therefore, there should be time given over to teachers from both phases observing specific lessons in each other's classes, perhaps engaging in joint teaching or joint classes of Year 6 and Year 7 pupils. It might also be worthwhile to target specific pre-negotiated issues, such as how special needs children are supported, how teacher assessment is conducted and how resources are used. Working together, Year 6 and Year 7 teachers can develop materials that can be used as a baseline for assessing pupils' attainment, helping at the same time to build a shared understanding of the various levels of achievement between the two types of schools.

Transfer of information

One vital element of good transition collaboration is the timely transfer of relevant information from the feeder primary schools to their partner secondary schools. Agreement on the scheduling of the transfer of information is crucial. A degree of compromise and understanding will often be required. Secondary schools will need to understand the pressure on primary schools to complete teacher assessment and end-of-Key Stage teacher assessments while primary schools will need to understand the importance secondary schools attach to having the results as early as possible to enable them to draw up their induction plans and first term activities. Agreement on the format of the information, i.e. the manner in which it is presented and delivered, should be a decision of the collaborating group but it may also be governed by external authorities. The partners are also more likely, as time goes on, to identify convenient electronic means of transferring information and of making it more accessible to more teachers in each school.

The final ingredient in the effective transfer of information is the relevance of the material transferred. To some extent this will be determined relatively easily by the secondary school stating the nature of the information that it requires and the form in which it requires it. However, a more important dimension will tend to be the interpretation of the National Curriculum assessment levels that make up some of the performance-based information. If, for example, the interpretation of Level 4 between the primary and secondary partners is very different, there will be the potential for misunderstandings and, worse, errors in planning for the pupils' progression in the subjects concerned. Some form of 'agreement trial' or moderation meetings between the Year 6 and Year 7 teachers will therefore be important in order to generate a shared understanding of assessment levels between the partners. In all of these matters, school managers will need to consider how they can enable sufficient time to be set aside for the teachers concerned to carry out the work involved.

A summary of recommendations for engaging schools in collaborative action on the transfer of information might include:

- primary–secondary standardization meetings are held between teachers of Year 6 and Year 7, pre- and post-transfer, to develop a shared understanding of levels of performance that pupils reach at the point of transfer;
- record-keeping systems are reviewed to ensure that all schools in the area use the same approach and presentation;
- agreements are reached on the nature and projected use of transfer information;
- agreement is reached on a timetable for passing records to pupils' new schools;
- consideration is given to how Year 7 teachers may find the time needed to review incoming records for planning lesson content and schemes of work;
- the system for transferring information is regularly reviewed in the light of feedback from parents, pupils and teachers;
- consideration is given to an electronic system for information transfer.

Liaison

Liaison between secondary schools and their feeder primary schools is a central feature of the collaborative framework and will not be rehearsed here; what is worth mentioning again, however, is the liaison needed between the partner schools and the transfer pupils and their parents. Parents are a key group in the collaborative network, without whose commitment and support so much of the good work undertaken by the schools can be quickly undone. If they are going to help their children to make informed decisions about the choice of secondary schools, parents need to know about transfer procedures from a very early stage. They will want to know how schools will induct their children and organize their learning. Primary schools can facilitate this by ensuring that parents have user-friendly documentation about the secondary schools on offer, and clearly the secondary schools must provide the documentation. Parents need to feel part of the transfer process and they will wish to be consulted at the various stages of transfer.

Pupils are another key focus for liaison arrangements and carefully planned induction measures. As with their parents, Year 6 pupils will want to look around their prospective new school or schools if they have a choice and are undecided. Once their school is decided they will appreciate the chance to meet their new teachers and even take part in sample lessons before they actually join the school. They will want to know about homework policies, about school rules and about day-to-day organizational matters such as lunch and other breaks. They will also want to know more about the life of the school, its sporting activities and its facilities.

In relation to parents and pupils then, collaborative action on liaison might include:

- secondary schools sending, to feeder primary schools, pamphlet-type information about themselves and about transition and induction arrangements, early in the transfer process;
- primary schools inviting parents to meetings early in Year 6 to discuss the transfer arrangement details and the options open to their children;
- parents being invited to secondary schools on open evenings early in Year 6 to see the schools for themselves;
- induction events for new pupils and their parents, just prior to the start of the school year, to introduce the new teachers and provide opportunities to find out more about the school.

The various activities necessary to underpin a successful collaboration on transition will need to be planned carefully in an agreed calendar of events and the next section considers a typical plan.

A calendar for action

The success of any collaborative network will depend crucially on good planning and an achievable calendar of action and events. Schools in a collaborative network will therefore need to establish a programme that maximizes the opportunities for cooperation and the availability of people and facilities. Even neighbouring schools may show wide variation in the way they organize their year but for most schools the high activity periods will commonly focus around seasonal festivals and, in recent times, external testing programmes. Some activities, such as Christmas plays, will occur around the same time and in some cases the similar timing will prove useful. In other cases, schedule clashes will present difficulties. For a collaborative programme to run smoothly there must be year-on-year planning with major joint events booked into the calendar well in advance of them happening. It is difficult to set down a template for a typical collaborative calendar but once agreement has been reached on the types of joint activity, the following will give some leads. Schools wishing to set their own timetable of events will wish to take account of the many local variations and needs that are possible.

March–April Easter time may well present some opportunities for collaborative planning on the main dates and events for the next year. Schools might therefore find it possible and beneficial to hold a meeting of liaison teachers around this time, with a draft timetable for the next year as the main agenda item.

Secondary schools, including schools in selective areas, will begin to have their next year's intake settled around this time and initial plans for familiarization or 'taster' days will need to be made.

May–June   Schools will want to work around external testing programmes (end of Key Stage, SATs etc.) to provide the planned 'taster' days and to engage in teacher exchange visits. As soon as it is possible, teacher assessments and SAT scores will be sent from the primary schools to the secondary schools to enable the induction teachers to begin their planning.

June–July   The end of the year is the ideal time to assess the previous year's joint activities and to polish off the planning of dates for the coming year. Several different people need to be involved: heads of core subjects, Year 7 teachers and Year 6 teachers will need to coordinate the curriculum issues (including those for the coming year), Year 7 and Year 6 teachers will need to coordinate dates and plans for any proposed joint teaching and visits, and liaison teachers will need to coordinate dates and plans for staff and pupil visits as part of any agreed orientation and induction programmes. Induction teachers in the secondary schools will be anxious to get as much information as possible on the incoming pupils to enable them to organize the class groupings and any setting or streaming that is involved.

August   The main holiday month, particularly the latter end of it, may well prove attractive to schools wishing to organize 'first year only' days, perhaps supported by volunteering older pupils. The purpose of these days would be largely social (the new Year 7s get to know each other) but will also serve to accustom the new pupils to the physical layout and facilities of the school.

September   The start of the year will be a busy period but several aspects will need attention. Headteachers of partner schools will want to meet to confirm the final planning for the year's programme while the heads of lower schools will want to begin their visits to their feeder primary schools to renew contact and discuss plans for transfer and induction arrangements for coming year.

October–November   These months will see the new school year reasonably settled and will enable the primary schools to begin preparation for the transfer process. This might involve an initial Year 6 parents' evening designed to give parents the opportunity to be informed about the arrangements for transfer and the choice of secondary schools in the area. They should also get the chance to meet representatives from these schools. The secondary schools will tend to arrange their first Year 7 parents' evening; as part of the induction programme and with the aim of discussing the settling in and progress of the new pupils. There may also be some opportunity in these months for continuing Year 6/7 teachers' curriculum planning meetings and for some teacher exchange visits.

December   Late December is 'no-go' for most collaborative activities but the early part of the month may well prove a good time for secondary schools to have an open day or evening to bring potential new pupils and their parents in to see around the school, talk to teachers and so on. The growing festive spirit and the various preparations for Christmas plays and carol services may well prove an attractive backdrop for introducing prospective pupils to the ambience of the school. Joint Christmas activities, such as plays or carol services involving the partner schools, will prove a valuable shop window for the collaboration in the community.

January–March   This time of year will witness the main pressure from parents and pupils in terms of deciding to which schools they want to transfer. Selection testing, where it exists, will also add greatly to the pressure on primary schools. Schools and parents will tend to receive notice of pupil placements towards the end of this period and primary schools may come under some pressure to forward initial teacher assessments to their partner secondary schools. Collaborative agreements on transfer arrangements will prove their worth as schools cope with this anxious time for pupils and parents.

Summary

A successful collaborative network, designed to pool the resources of partner schools in the pursuit of a smooth transition from Key Stage 2 to 3, will require regular attention to the many tasks and objectives involved. Although not exhaustive, the following checklist will assist in assessing the extent to which any network is meeting its objectives:

- key people in the partner schools are known to each other and visit each other for liaison and, ideally, joint teaching purposes;
- continuity in the content of Year 6 and 7 curricula is agreed between the partner schools;
- overlap in specific resource and experiential areas, for example in the choice of books for literature and reading work or the choice of experiments for science, is kept to a minimum;
- gaps in the delivery of the Key Stage 2 curriculum, which acts as the basis on which to build Key Stage 3, are kept to a minimum;
- the interpretation of standards (levels) of pupil achievement is shared between the partner schools in both phases;

- dissemination of information to enable pupils and parents to choose their next schools is sufficiently informative and timely;
- the transfer of information from primary schools is sufficiently informative and timely for the secondary schools to induct pupils at accurate levels of achievement and, where possible, in class groupings that capitalize on friendships between pupils coming from the same feeder schools;
- Year 6 pupils, and their parents, are provided with orientation and induction programmes to assist them in acclimatizing to the changes experienced in moving to Year 7;
- an anxiety-free induction to secondary school life, especially in the first few days, is top priority.

Bibliography

ATL (1996) *Doing Our Level Best: An Evaluation of Statutory Assessment in 1995*. London: Association of Teachers and Lecturers.

Bullock Report (1975) *A Language for Life*, London: HMSO.

Cockcroft Report (1982) *Mathematics Counts*. Report of the Committee of Inquiry into the Teaching of Mathematics in Schools, London: HMSO.

Crone, R. and Malone, J. (1979) *Continuities in Education: The Northern Ireland Schools Curriculum Project*. Windsor: NFER Nelson.

Dawson, R. and Shipstone, D. (1991) 'Liaison in science at the primary/secondary interface'. *School Science Review* 72 (261): 17–25.

Dean, J. (1988) 'Continuity'. In M. Clarkson (ed.) *Emerging Issues in Primary Education*. London: Falmer, 90–8.

Derricott, R. (ed.) (1985) *Primary to Secondary, Curriculum Continuity and School Organisation*, Slough: NFER-Nelson.

DES (1989) *Education Observed 10: Curriculum Continuity at 11-plus: continuity of learning in a sample of primary and secondary schools in England*. London: HMSO.

DES/WO (1987) 'The National Curriculum 5–16: A Consultation Document', London and Cardiff: Department of Education and Science, and the Welsh Office.

DFE (1995) *The National Curriculum*. Department for Education, London: HMSO.

DfEE (1997) 'Proposed Arrangements for Collecting Statistical Information from Schools', Section 2: 'Unique pupil numbers', London: Department for Education and Employment.

Doyle, L. (1997) *Bridging the Gap: Liaison Procedures for Curriculum Continuity at Key Stage 2/3 Transfer: Teacher Research Award Report*, Teacher Training Agency, London: Stagg House/TTA.

Gorwood, B. (1989) 'Experience of problems relative to curriculum continuity and school transfer in teacher-training courses'. In V.A. McClelland and V.P. Varma (eds) *Advances in Teacher Education*. London: Routledge, 71–102.

—— (1994) 'Primary–secondary transfer after the National Curriculum'. In R. Moon and A.S. Mayes (eds) *Teaching and Learning in the Secondary School*. London: Routledge (in association with the Open University), 357–61.

Griffiths, J. and Jones, L. (1994) 'And you have to dissect frogs!'. *Forum* 36 (3): 83–4.

Hadow Report (1931), London: HMSO.

Hargreaves, A. and Earl, L. (1990) *Rights of Passage: A Review of Selected Research about Schooling in the Transition Years*. Report to Ontario Ministry of Education, Toronto: MGS Publications.

Harlen, W. (1995) *Putting 5–14 in place: an overview of the methods and findings of the evaluation, 1991–95*, Interchange No. 35, Edinburgh: The Scottish Office Education and Industry Department, Research and Intelligence Unit.

Hughes, M. (ed.) (1994) *Progression in Learning*, BERA Dialogues 11, Clevedon: Multilingual Matters Ltd.

Jarman, R. (1993) 'Real experiments with bunsen burners: pupils' perceptions of similarities and differences between primary science and secondary science'. School Science Review 74 (268): 19–29.

—— (1997) 'Fine in theory: a study of primary–secondary continuity in science, prior and subsequent to the introduction of the Northern Ireland Curriculum'. *Educational Research* 39 (3): 291–310.

Jones, L. (1995) 'Continuity in the curriculum'. *Forum* 37 (2): 44–6.

Lance, A. (1994) 'The case for continuity'. *Forum* 36 (2): 46–7.

—— (1995) 'Transferring to secondary school: whose choice?'. *Forum* 37 (2): 46–7.

McKibben, J.A. and Sutherland, A.E. (1992) *From the Receiving End: Evidence from Post-Primary Principals*. Belfast: Northern Ireland Council for Educational Research.

Millar, R., Gott, R., Lubben, F. and Duggan, S. (1994) 'Children's performance of investigative tasks in science: a framework for considering progression'. In M. Hughes (ed.) *Progression in Learning*, BERA Dialogues 11, Clevedon: Multilingual Matters Ltd., 82–108.

Munn, P. (1994) 'Progression in learning; literacy and numeracy in the pre-school'. In M. Hughes (ed.) *Progression in Learning*, BERA Dialogues 11, Clevedon: Multilingual Matters Ltd., 15–23.

Naylor, J. (1990) 'Across the great divide: an experiment in liaison'. *Education 3–13* (June): 55–9.

OFSTED (1995) *Science: A Review of Inspection Findings 1993/4*. Office for Standards in Education, London: HMSO.

Plowden Report (1967) *Children and their Primary Schools*. A Report of the Central Advisory Council for Education (England), vol. 1, London: HMSO.

SCAA (1996) *Monitoring the School Curriculum: Reporting to Schools*. London: School Curriculum and Assessment Authority.

—— (1997) *Making Effective Use of Key Stage 2 Assessments at the Transfer between Key Stage 2 and Key Stage 3 to Support Teaching of Pupils in Year 7*. London: School Curriculum and Assessment Authority.

Schagen, S. and Kerr, D. (1997) 'Curriculum continuity: reality or myth?' Paper disseminated at the British Educational Research Association Annual Conference in York.

Simon, S., Brown, M., Black, P. and Blondel, E. (1994) 'Progression in learning mathematics and science', in M. Hughes (ed.) *Progression in Learning*, BERA Dialogues 11, Clevedon: Multilingual Matters Ltd., 24–49.

Speering, W. and Rennie, L. (1996) 'Students' perceptions about science: The impact of transition from primary to secondary school'. *Research in Science Education* 26 (3): 283–98.

Squires, K. (1994) 'Moving on: the poetry of transition'. *English in Education* 28 (2): 31–5.

Stillman, A. and Maychell, K. (1984) *School to School: LEA and Teacher Involvement in Educational Continuity*. Windsor: NFER Nelson.

Sutherland, A., Johnston, L. and Gardner, J. (1996) *The Transition between Key Stage 2 and Key Stage 3: A Report for the Northern Ireland Council for Curriculum, Examinations and Assessment*. Belfast: NICCEA.

Tabor, D.C. (1990) 'Poetry across the divide'. *Education 3–13* (March): 33–40.

Talbot, C. (1990) 'When the talking stops'. *Education 3–13* (March): 28–32.

Tickle, L. (1985) 'From class teacher to specialist teacher'. In R. Derricot (ed.) *Primary to Secondary, Curriculum Continuity and School Organisation*, Slough: NFER-Nelson.

Tuckman, B.W. (1985) in R. Derricott (ed.) *Primary to Secondary, Curriculum Continuity and School Organisation*, Slough: NFER-Nelson.

Vickery, D. (1987) 'Teachers' views of progression in science'. *Primary Science Review* 5: 24–5.

Weston, P., Barrett, E. and Jamison, J. (1992) *The Quest for Coherence: Managing the Whole Curriculum*, Slough: NFER.

Whittaker, M. (1980) 'They're only playing: the problem of primary science'. *School Science Review* 61 (216): 556–60.

Williams, M. and Howley, R. (1989) 'Curriculum discontinuity: a study of a secondary school and its feeder primary schools'. *British Educational Research Journal* 15 (1): 61–76.

Williams, M. and Jephcote, M. (1993) 'Continuities and discontinuities in economic and industrial understanding between the primary and secondary phases'. *School Organisation* 13 (1): 61–71.

Index